Animals and Plants That Trap

Animals and Plants That Trap

Philip Goldstein

ILLUSTRATED BY MATTHEW KALMENOFF

Holiday House · New York

To Michael and Bobby, for whom this book was written: I hope you enjoy reading about The Trappers as much as I enjoyed writing about them.

Grandpa Phil

Text copyright © 1974 by Philip Goldstein.
Illustrations copyright © 1974 by Holiday House, Inc.
All rights reserved.
Printed in the United States of America.

Library of Congress Cataloging in Publication Data

Goldstein, Philip, 1910–
    Animals and plants that trap.

    SUMMARY: Describes the habits and special characteristics of various plants and animals that survive by trapping their prey.
    Bibliography: p.
    1. Animals, Food habits of—Juvenile literature.
2. Insectivorous plants—Juvenile literature.
[1. Animals—Food habits. 2. Insectiverous plants. 3. Plants]
I. Kalmenoff, Matthew, illus. II. Title.
QL756.5.G64   574.5'3   73–16874
ISBN: 0–8234–0241–X

Contents

1
A Better Mousetrap

It is an old story. If you build a better mousetrap, the world will beat a path to your door. But what makes your mousetrap better than those already in existence?

Does your new trap attract more mice than the old-style traps? Is it so beautifully camouflaged that even cautious mice are fooled into thinking it is harmless? Perhaps your trap is designed so cleverly that even the smartest mouse in the whole world cannot steal the bait. Maybe you added some little device that holds the captured mice more securely.

Whatever change you made in the trap gave it a big advantage. The new trap did the job better than the old conventional ones. As word got around, more and more people began to buy your improved mousetrap. Why should they spend money on traps that don't work nearly as well as yours? Other kinds of traps gradually disappeared from the marketplace. But your new, improved mousetrap flourished and increased.

Adaptations are a basic part of every animal. Porpoises are adapted for swimming swiftly through water because their bodies are thoroughly streamlined. If by some magic they were suddenly turned into squarish animals with rough skin, they probably could not catch enough fish to survive.

In a manner of speaking, we can say that your trap was better *adapted* to survive in the market competition. The word "adapted" comes from the Latin *adaptare*, which means "to fit." Why was your trap fit to survive? Because it had some special structure that made it better. Or because it functioned more efficiently than other traps.

Now let us make an analogy to living things. This world of ours is a dangerous place. Plants and animals are under constant pressure from predators, overcrowding, man's hunting and making harmful changes in the environment, and other dangers. One mistake can lead to death. And yet animals and plants continue to survive generation after generation. What is the secret of their success?

Perhaps we can compare a successful organism to our better mousetrap. The trap was better adapted to survive in the competition of the marketplace. And the organism was better adapted to survive in the competition of life. Adaptation is the answer to our question.

2
Adaptation—the Secret of Survival

An adaptation is any feature of a living thing that helps it to achieve the two great necessities of life. First, the organism must stay alive as an individual. Second, it must reproduce so that its species will continue into the next generation.

Sometimes an adaptation is a special organ, tissue, or process that makes an animal or plant especially fit to do some particular thing. Thus the wings of a bird are an adaptation for flying. This special ability helps the bird to stay alive.

On the other hand, an adaptation may help the living thing to produce others like itself. For example, certain kinds of bacteria can produce spores when living conditions turn unfavorable. These are tough, dry cells that survive the bad conditions and sprout again when things get better. Bacteria that cannot form spores are usually killed by the unfavorable conditions. But the spore-formers survive and carry through to the next generation.

Another form of adaptation is the power to adjust to changes in conditions. Thus a dog grows a heavier coat in the wintertime when it is cold; when it gets warm again he sheds the excess hair.

Some adaptations have to do with the way an organism behaves. For example, the leaves of a green plant always turn toward the light. The stem of a plant tends to grow upwards against the pull of gravity. The roots usually grow toward a source of water.

Can you see how these special organs and abilities help the living thing to stay alive? Can you add other examples that you yourself have noticed in various animals or plants?

Some adaptations may seem startling. People crossing the Gulf of Mexico for the first time are often surprised to see flying fish shoot out of the water

A young flying fish attempting to take off in an aquarium. When it has the freedom of the ocean it leaps through the water surface and glides through the air on its winglike front fins, one of many surprising adaptations among fish.

DR. WILLIAM M. STEPHENS

like so many arrows. "How can fish fly?" they ask. Flying fish don't really fly, but they cover a lot of territory in each jump. These fish have a special adaptation in the form of greatly enlarged fins that look almost like wings. But they do not flap them; they spread them out wide and so get support in gliding through the air. By beating its tail vigorously, a flying fish can sail several hundred yards before it falls back into the water.

You may think this is a useless and even silly adaptation. But that spectacular jump is a way of escaping from a pursuing enemy. The enlargement of the fins is a valuable life-saving device.

Not all adaptations are as unusual as this one. They ordinarily go unnoticed. Do you realize how many separate adaptations go into making your hand the efficient organ that it is? Take a good look at your palm. Why is it crisscrossed with all those deep lines and furrows? Are they there by accident? Those creases are wonderful adaptations that help your hand to function efficiently. Close your hand partly without bending your fingers. Do you see how the skin of your palm and the tissues below the skin fold along those creases? If your skin were stiff and uncreased, could you close your hand?

Now study your fingers for a minute. Bend them slowly and straighten them again. Do you see how neatly the tissues on the underside fold up as the joint bends? Now hold your fingers straight out and ex-

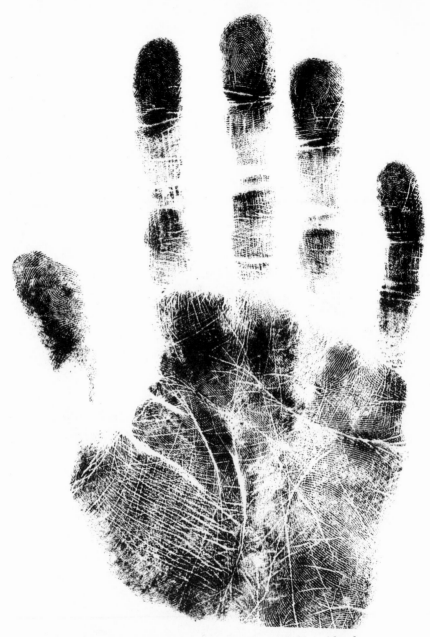

The human hand, with its creased, flexible, slidable, ridged skin, is a wonderful example of biological adaptation.

amine the backs of them. Notice the folds of skin over the joints. What happens to these folds when you clench your fist?

Open your hand again. The skin on the back of the hand is quite loose. You can pinch it up easily with the fingers of your other hand. But make a fist and try to grasp the skin again. What happened to the loose skin?

All these creases and loose folds are important adaptations for the functioning of your hand. And there are still more. Look closely at the skin on your palm and your fingers. Notice that the entire surface is covered with tiny ridges curving and turning in every direction. (You can get a clearer view with a magnifying glass.) The ridges are everywhere but they are most prominent on your fingertips. There they form a series of fancy curves and arches.

You may say they are your fingerprints, but they are not there to identify you. They are called friction ridges, because they prevent slipping when you grasp something. Thus your hand becomes a more efficient tool. It is really a bundle made up of many adaptations.

If that is true of your hand, then your whole body must be a superbundle of such helps toward working efficiently. So it is—and you go through life without realizing that all those adaptations exist. But they are there working for you every minute. They worked for your ancestors too, enabling them to stay

Friction ridges of a human thumb, shown enlarged

alive and produce you. They keep you alive in turn and will help you to participate in producing the next generation of humans.

Every living organism is a superbundle of adaptations. The bundle is vast and complex. Each separate adaptation is involved with one little part of life. But taken together, the many hundreds of them make for overall biological success. No person can unravel and understand all the adaptations in any one plant or animal. Usually we recognize only a few of the obvious ones, those that are the most unusual. Consider, for example, the plant called the wake-robin.

3
An Unusual Insect Trap

Many plants have reproductive organs called flowers. For reproduction to occur, the female parts of the flower must be dusted with pollen from the male parts. This process is called pollination. Each plant has its own special way of accomplishing it. But of all the techniques that are used, there is none as surprising as that of the wake-robin, sometimes called the cuckoo-pint.

The wake-robin is a European plant related to the American jack-in-the-pulpit. It has separate male and female flowers. The female flowers cluster on a stalk at the bottom of a cuplike well. The male flowers are located in a separate cluster a little higher on the same stalk. Still higher up, a cluster of stiff downward-pointing hairs guards the entrance to the cup. The stalk then continues upward out of the cup to form a heavy club-shaped structure.

The female flowers in the cup ripen first. When they do, the plant begins to give off an aroma like

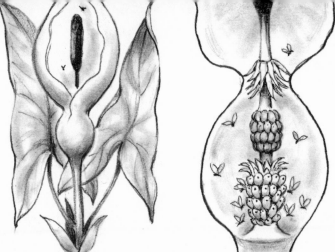

ABOVE: *The wake-robin gives off a disagreeable smell which is, however, attractive to certain insects. At right the spathe, or bulbous portion, is cut open to show insects, covered with the pollen from another wake-robin, trapped inside by spikes in the narrow neck. As they fly around, the pollen rubs off on the stigmas—the pollen-receiving organs—which pass it on to the ovules.*

BELOW: *The ovules—rounded outgrowths that develop into seed—have been fertilized and are growing larger. Meanwhile, the anthers above them, which produce pollen, have burst and the pollen falls on the insects. The spikes droop, allowing the insects to escape and fly to some other plant of this species to repeat the process.*

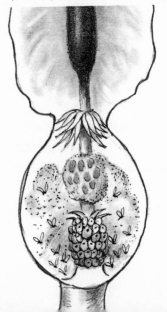

that of decaying animal wastes. This is most attractive to certain flies and beetles that depend on animal wastes for their food.

This alluring odor serves as bait. It invites the insects to enter the cup in search of food. They start climbing downward. Suddenly the footing becomes very slippery. The surface is covered with droplets of an oily substance.

The insects skid downward. They slip by the downward-pointing hairs and fall to the bottom of the well. And now they cannot get out. The sides of the cup are as smooth as glass. The exit at the top is guarded by the ring of hairs. The insects are trapped. They spend the rest of the day running around near the bottom of the cup. They crawl all over the female flowers. They make frantic efforts to escape, but without success.

During the night the male flowers open. Showers of pollen drop down on the captive insects below. At the same time, the walls of the prison begin to dry out and become rough enough for a foothold. The stiff hairs at the top wither away. By next morning the pollen-covered prisoners are able to sneak out of the trap.

However, they do not seem to learn from their experience. They are soon attracted by the aroma of another cuckoopint plant whose female flowers have ripened. They cannot resist the odor. They are trapped again.

Once more they dash frantically around the bottom of the cup. As they brush against the ripe female flowers, the pollen they are carrying rubs off. Pollination has been accomplished.

Can you think of a better "mousetrap"? The plant baits its trap with an odor that the insects cannot resist. It catches them and holds them captive until they perform a task that helps the plant reproduce. And then the prisoners are released unharmed.

Perhaps you are surprised by the fact that a plant can be a trapper. But long before man even existed on this earth, various kinds of plants and animals were setting traps that catch prey, or that bring about reproduction, and they are still doing it today.

4
A Very Effective Pitfall

As night begins to fall, a delicate insect with long gauzy wings comes into view. It hovers awkwardly over the shrubbery like a lazy helicopter. It is hunting for the tiny insects on which it feeds.

This flying machine looks very much like a damselfly with its long body and four delicate wings. But it is a related insect with a name that is even longer than its body—*Myrmeleon formicarius*. This delicate, lazy-winged insect is the mother of the not-so-delicate ant lion. She flies about from June to September. As summer draws to a close, she looks for a sandy place that is protected against the rain. There she drops her precious eggs. These eggs must produce the next generation.

They remain buried in the sand through the winter cold, and hatch when the warmth of spring arrives. But the creature that emerges from the egg is not at all like its mother. It is an ugly, wingless little thing; its heavy gray body is covered with warts and bristles. There is a rounded abdomen, a short movable neck, and a large squarish head.

The most prominent feature on the head is a long pair of curving jaws covered with jagged teeth. These jaws are sharply pointed. A hollow canal runs through each jaw, from the pointed tip all the way to the head.

This miniature monster is known as an ant lion, sometimes as a doodlebug. The very name tells you

If you were the size of an ant, an ant lion would look like quite a monster.

that it must be an ant-killer. One can also guess that those toothed jaws are a special adaptation for grasping a struggling ant. However, before it can grip its victim, it must first catch the ant. Ants are very agile and run about quickly on their long legs. This puts the awkward, clumsy ant lion at a disadvantage. It cannot run nearly as well as the prey that it must catch.

Long, long ago, the ancestors of modern ant lions learned to build an ant trap. We don't know how they first developed this unusual pattern of behavior, or when it happened. And we certainly don't understand how the behavior pattern is passed on from one generation to the next. The newly hatched ant lion couldn't possibly learn the trick from its mother, which it never even sees. However, we do know how the young insect builds its trap.

When it hatches from the egg, it is a hungry little thing. Fast work is necessary to satisfy its hunger. The trap in which victims will be captured must be built in a hurry. The ant lion chooses a likely spot in the sandy location where its mother laid the egg. Then it begins to work.

First it marks off a circular groove. (It is amazing that this tiny insect can draw such a perfect circle.) Then it starts at the edge of the circle and backs up toward the center. It uses its heavy body like a plow to shovel the sand backward. With a front leg it heaps the loose sand on its head. Then with a sudden jerk it tosses the sand right out of the circle.

Round and round goes the ant lion, from the circle inward toward the middle. Soon the trap begins to take shape. It is a sand pit with very steep sides. The walls are so steep that the grains of sand just barely stay in place. The slightest touch will send them tumbling downward.

When the trap is completed, the ant lion digs itself into the sand at the bottom. It is completely hidden from view—only the piercing jaws stick out. In this position it waits. Any crawling insect that dares go over the edge of the trap is fair game.

Let us watch an ant as it scurries this way and that, exploring as it goes. Without realizing the danger, the ant steps over the edge of the pit. It takes a step in the loose sand, then another. Suddenly the grains of sand give way. Each one rolls like a marble beneath its feet. Even with six powerful legs, the ant cannot seem to gain a foothold. It begins to slip and slide.

Sometimes the intended victim manages to regain its footing and begins to climb upward out of the pit. Then the ant lion uses another trick. It jerks its head and tosses showers of sand ahead of the struggling ant. These set off miniature landslides. The victim's footing is undermined and he goes tumbling backward.

The jaws of the ant lion grab the victim and their sharp points pierce its body. Now the ant lion pumps digestive fluids through the hollow canals in the jaws, and they enter the body of the victim. Thus digestion is carried out in the body of the prey rather than inside

Any ant that manages to climb back up again is likely to be defeated by showers of sand.

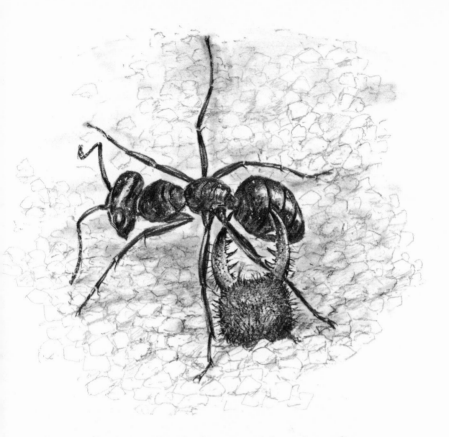

The ant lion's jaws are both spears and suction tubes—a highly efficient adaptation.

the ant lion. After a while everything digestible in the ant is turned into a fluid. Now the ant lion sucks in the nutritious fluid through the same hollow canals of the jaws.

The ant lion gets nutrients from its victim but it never takes any waste material into its body—a very efficient system. Soon the victim is sucked dry. Now the ant lion sticks its head under the lifeless skin and with a quick jerk it tosses the lifeless body out of the pit. Quickly the insect smoothes the sides of the trap. Once again it buries itself in the sand at the bottom. The trap has been reset, and the trapper is ready for another victim.

Nobody can say how many ants a doodlebug eats in its lifetime. But as it eats it grows, and the larger it grows, the larger it can make the trap. When the ant lion reaches its full growth, the funnel may measure three inches across at the top, and two inches deep.

An ant lion takes anywhere from one to three years to change into a flying adult. Now it loses interest in catching any more ants. It digs down to a depth of about four inches into the sand and forms a cocoon. This looks like a round ball of sand stuck together with fine silk. It is about the size of a large pea. Of course it is a hollow ball, with the ant lion inside.

The cocoon is formed sometime around May. Inside it mysterious things take place that change the insect into the delicate, winged adult. In about a month the changes are complete. The adult gnaws its way out of the cocoon. A cycle of one generation has been completed. Now, like a slowly moving helicopter this new adult will hover over the vegetation. It will feed on tiny insects. Later that summer eggs will be laid, and the whole story will be repeated.

Do you want to see an ant lion in action? There are about 60 different species widely distributed over the United States. They may be found in almost any

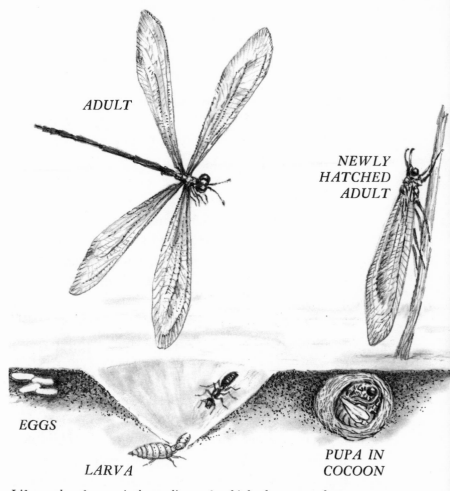

ADULT

NEWLY HATCHED ADULT

EGGS

LARVA

PUPA IN COCOON

Life cycle of a typical ant lion, of which there are about 650 species

sandy area but especially in the dry parts of the South. Look for them in warm, dry, sandy, protected places. Keep your eyes wide open and look for the telltale circular pits with the steep walls. Perhaps the doodlebug will be sitting there with its jaws sticking out. Perhaps it will be buried in the sand, so that nothing is visible.

There is an old-time notion that you can trick the doodlebug into coming out of its hiding place. All you have to do is lean over the pit and say "Doodle—doodle—doodle." If you try this trick, let your breath hit hard against the sides of the pit. Perhaps this will blow some sand particles and make them tumble down. Then the doodlebug may stick out its head to catch the ant it expects to find sliding down.

If you see the ant lion sitting at the bottom of the pit, you may be able to capture it with a straw. If it grabs at the straw with its jaws, you can lift it out. Or you can use a spoon to scoop up the sand just below the bottom of the funnel. If you empty it onto a sheet of white paper, you will know soon enough whether or not you captured an ant lion.

If you capture one, treat it gently. Take it home and give it clean, dry sand in a deep pan or a large jar. Then you can watch the building of a trap. However, if you do make a pet of an ant lion, you must be prepared to provide it with plenty of live ants to eat. If you keep count, maybe you will be able to determine how many ants it can eat in a day.

Before you leave this unusual trapper and its pit, give this question a little thought: how many adaptations can you figure out that relate to constructing the trap and to capturing prey?

5
The Snap-Trap of Venus

In the 1800s, travelers returning from unexplored tropical islands brought back many strange stories of "man-eating plants." For example, a certain sea captain reported that he had seen a "devil flower" somewhere in the South Pacific. According to his story this was a huge flower, with beautiful coloring and fragrance. It was so large that a man could walk right into its hollow part. Once he entered the beautifully colored trap he was lost. The perfume put him to sleep, and the flower folded its petals over him. He was never seen again.

Another traveler said that he had seen a "snake tree" with sensitive, snakelike branches. If a bird landed on a branch of this tree, it was grasped by the branches and drawn down into the interior. He said that when one of his traveling companions touched a branch, his hand was grasped so tightly that the skin was ripped.

Someone else told about a man-eating tree that

was considered sacred by the natives. From time to time they gave it a beautiful maiden as a sacrifice. He even insisted that he had witnessed such an event. The tree, he said, looked like an oversized pineapple, with a barrel-shaped trunk ten feet tall. A ring of leaves hung down from the top. Each leaf was ten to twelve feet long and a foot wide. The entire leaf was covered with evil-looking, poisonous thorns. When the victim was presented to the tree the leaves suddenly came to life. They began to twist and turn and wrap themselves around the victim. They pressed their thorns into the poor girl with such force that she was killed.

These are certainly remarkable stories. They aroused the interest of all who heard them. They were published in newspapers, magazines, and even in scientific journals. However, when biologists actually went searching for these man-traps, they were nowhere to be found. To this day, nobody has discovered a real man-eating plant.

Still, truth is considered to be stranger than fiction. Perhaps man-eating plants do not exist, but there are certainly many plants that eat insects. Biologists know over 450 different kinds of plants that do this. Their trapping methods are perhaps more ingenious and more complicated than anything a science-fiction writer would imagine.

Most trapper-plants live in bogs and marshes where the soil lacks certain minerals. Plants usually do not grow well without these minerals. However, the insect-trappers can thrive because they get the needed chemicals from their victims. Experiments show that the plants can actually survive without insect prey—but with it they grow bigger, better, and healthier.

The trappers of the plant world use many different kinds of mechanisms. One of the most unusual is the "snap-trap" used by Venus's-flytrap. It is a small plant with a rather poor root system. Its leaves form a small rosette that hugs the ground. When the plant grows in strong sunlight the leaves turn bright red. Otherwise they remain green.

When you look at one, a striking feature immediately catches your eye. There are strange-looking lobes at the ends of the leaves. Each lobe is decorated with a fringe of hairlike teeth along the edges. These are the snap-traps for which the plant is famous. They are among the most unusual structures in the entire plant world.

As you can readily see in the picture, each trap has two rounded lobes, hinged at the middle. When the trap is open the lobes are separated at an angle of about 45°. You can clearly see the fringe of spikes, or teeth, along the outer edge of each lobe. Now locate a trap that is closed. Notice that the two lobes have squeezed together. The teeth along the margin have interlocked, like your fingers when you clasp your hands.

Venus's-flytrap is a trapper, not a hunter. It

Venus's-flytrap seen from above

cannot go out looking for prey. It can only sit where it is rooted, and "wait" for a victim to be lured to its trap.

Let's imagine that a fly has landed on the plant. It seems to be exploring, as though it is following a scent. That is exactly what it is doing. The lobes of the fly-trap have glands that secrete a fluid with an odor. Human beings can't smell it, but flies can. And they find it irresistible.

The fly, following the scent, has reached a trap at the end of a leaf. Now its head is inside. Now its body follows. Suddenly a surprising thing happens: the two lobes come together quickly. The teeth at the margins interlock. The fly is caught in a boxlike prison. The more it struggles, the tighter the two lobes squeeze together.

The fact that the trap can close fast enough to catch a fly amazes even trained scientists. It takes under half a second to lock the victim into its prison. How can a plant move that quickly? It has no nerves to transmit messages quickly, no muscles to pull the lobes shut.

Biologists have watched the trap close, measured its speed, and wondered. But so far nobody really knows how the plant does it. The best attempt at an explanation speaks of sudden changes in internal water pressure. The trap is supposed to be held open by high pressure. When an insect enters the trap, the water pressure is suddenly reduced, and the trap snaps shut. Whether the theory is right or wrong makes no difference to the plant. In its own quiet way it has been trapping insects for centuries.

As soon as the prey is captured, the lobes of the trap begin to give off digestive fluids. These attack the soft parts of the insect's body and convert them into products that the plant can absorb for its needs.

It may take from eight to ten days for digestion to be completed. The trap remains closed during all this time. However, eventually it opens again, and the useless remains are blown away by winds. The trap is now reset and ready to take in another victim.

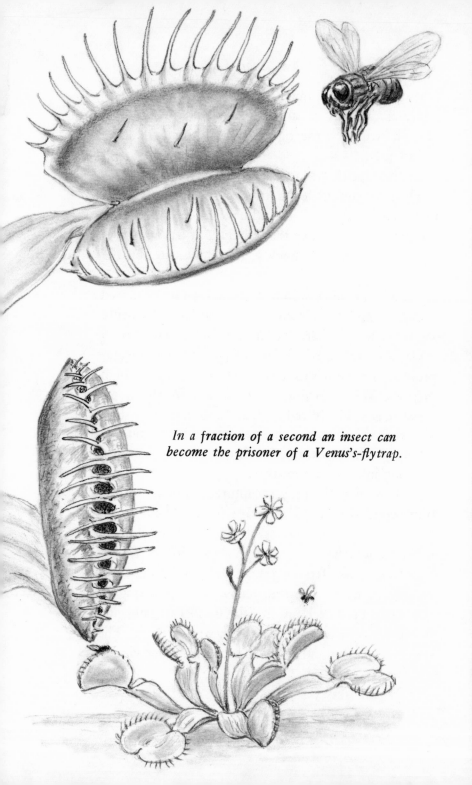

In a fraction of a second an insect can become the prisoner of a Venus's-flytrap.

Venus's-flytrap is an exciting plant to grow at home. You can buy bulbs of it from several biological-supply houses or from a company that specializes in insect-eating plants.* The bulbs should be planted in peat moss, sphagnum moss, vermiculite, or perlite. They do not need rich soil, but they do need lots of moisture. Keep the planting medium moist at all times, but don't make it soggy, since you shouldn't drown the plants.

The leafy traps will develop in three or four weeks after the bulbs are planted. Keep them in a sunny place. During the summer, put the planter outside from time to time. This will give the plants a chance to trap flies, mosquitoes, moths, and whatever small insects are around. The nutrients obtained from insects trapped during the summer are stored in the bulb and used at other times.

Once you have plants growing, you can carry out a variety of observations and experiments. For example, see if you can find the trigger hairs that set off the closing of the traps. Each lobe usually has three delicate bristles arranged in the form of a triangle. They may be hard to find, but you can see

* Carolina Biological Supply Co., Burlington, North Carolina 27215

General Biological Supply House (Turtox), 8200 South Hoyne Ave., Chicago, Illinois 60620

Insectivorous Botanic Garden, 1918 Market St., Wilmington, North Carolina 28401 them if you look very carefully. A hand lens is very helpful.

If you locate the triggers, see if you can fool the plants into closing the traps by touching them with a fine needle. Be sure you do this in a gentle way, with a light hand. Remember that an insect need only brush against these triggers with a leg to start the action. It is said that the trap requires a *double touch* to make it close. Either one hair must be touched twice in succession or two separate hairs must be touched once each. Does this mean that the plant can count?

If the plant "counts," can it also "remember"? Try touching a hair and then waiting a second or two before applying the second touch. Will the plant "remember" the first touch and still respond? Or do the two touches have to come in quick succession?

When an insect is captured, the trap stays closed for eight to ten days. What happens when you fool the trap into closing by touching the triggers? Does the trap stay closed for that length of time even if it is empty?

Carefully cut off a whole leaf with an open trap. Does the trap still respond when the trigger hairs are touched?

How many teeth are there on the margin of the trap? Is the number the same on all mature traps or is there a variation? Do young traps begin life with fewer teeth than they have when they are mature?

A couple of hundred years ago this remarkable plant was completely unknown to the botanists of the world. This is hardly surprising because its natural home is in a small area in North Carolina. It grows nowhere else in the whole world.

In 1760 Governor Arthur Dobbs of North Carolina sent a letter to a friend in England telling him about this unusual plant. Then in 1768 an American botanist sent a description of Venus's-flytrap to Carl Linnaeus in Europe. He also described the skill with which this trapper of the plant world captures insects.

Linnaeus, one of the most respected botanists of the time, could not bring himself to believe that a green, flowering plant could kill and eat insects. He thought that their capture was strictly accidental. It took another hundred years to establish Venus's-flytrap as a real trapper.

6
The Web of the Caddis Worm

If you happen to live near the shores of a lake or stream, you may be familiar with the caddis fly. It is a small, gray-brown, mothlike insect with long slender antennae (feelers). It is a weak little thing that hovers about on four lacy wings covered with fine hairs. It never wanders far from its watery home. If it comes to rest on a twig or a rock, it folds its wings straight back against its sides. The inner edges of the wings meet at the top to form a sort of tent over the body.

Caddis flies are not usually seen in the daytime. But after dark they cluster in large numbers around any light that shines out of the darkness. According to old records, caddis flies made it necessary to change the location of the Pan American Exhibit in 1901. Such large numbers of them were attracted to the electric lights at the exhibition site that they became a nuisance. In the end a new site had to be chosen farther inland from the Niagara River, which was the source of the insects.

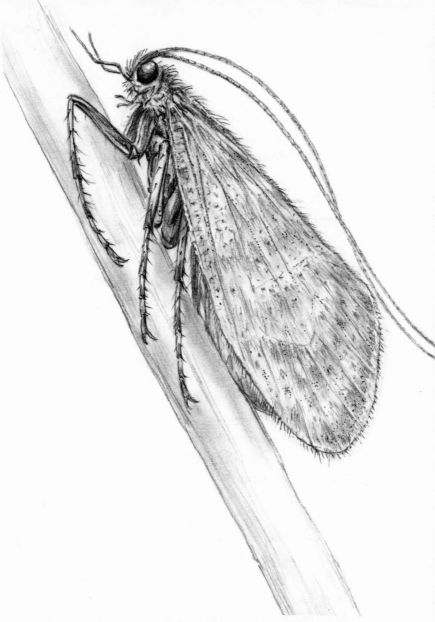

The adult caddis fly can walk swiftly but—in spite of its four large wings—is a rather weak flyer. It is active only in the nighttime, and can often be found around lights.

Aside from the annoyance they may cause as they cluster around lights, caddis flies are quite harmless. They may live from a week or so to several months. Some of them do not eat a thing during the entire period of adult life. Their main function is to reproduce, creating a new generation of caddis flies for next year.

The males and females mate in the air. Shortly thereafter the males die. The females live a little longer—long enough to deposit fertile eggs in the water. Then they too die. With egg-laying completed, the adults have played their part in assuring a new generation.

Caddis fly eggs do not hatch into winged insects like the parent. Rather they develop into little caterpillar-like creatures called caddis worms. Technically speaking, a caddis worm is the larval stage in the life history of the caddis fly. Of course it is not a worm.

While the adult caddis flies may sometimes be a nuisance to man, the larvae are of great importance as fish food. Hungry fish gobble up any and all caddis worms they can get hold of. But the caddis worms show adaptive behavior that helps protect them against fish, by making them less visible. Each worm builds itself a case or tube as a home in which to live.

Each variety of caddis worm has its own favorite building material: sand grains, tiny pebbles, bits of sticks, particles of plant material. These fragments are cemented together to form a special kind of case

Types of caddis-worm tubes →

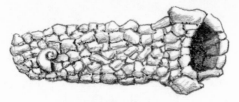

CYLINDER CASE

WINGED STICK CASE

BARK CASE

CHIMNEY CASE

LOG CABIN

or tube, like those in the illustration. The cementing material is fine silk, produced by the larva. Inside the tube it spins a smooth silk lining. However, the little creature is not safe anyway—many fish will gulp them down, tube and all.

One end of the caddis worm's tube is always left open, and the creature is able to stick out its head and legs. In this position it can crawl about on the bottom, dragging its house along. This is how it hunts for tiny water animals and plants to eat. Perhaps the caddis fly mother didn't have much of an appetite, but the larva never stops eating. It eats and grows, eats and grows.

There are many kinds of caddis worms that are trappers. For example, certain kinds fasten their houses firmly to a rock or to a plant. Then they crawl out cautiously and spin small webs of silk among the pebbles at the bottom. Next they return to the safety of the house. The little webs entangle various tiny water creatures. Later the caddis worm visits its traps and devours the victims it finds trapped there. In this way they act very much like human trappers who set out a whole series of traps and later remove any victims that were caught.

Other trappers among the caddis worms belong to the group called the water-net caddis flies. They live in flowing streams, where they spin large, funnel-shaped trap nets. Sometimes the funnel is as much as eight or nine inches long. As you see in the illustration, the trap net has a broad opening facing upstream.

Some caddis insects rival spiders in building well constructed, effective nets for gathering food.

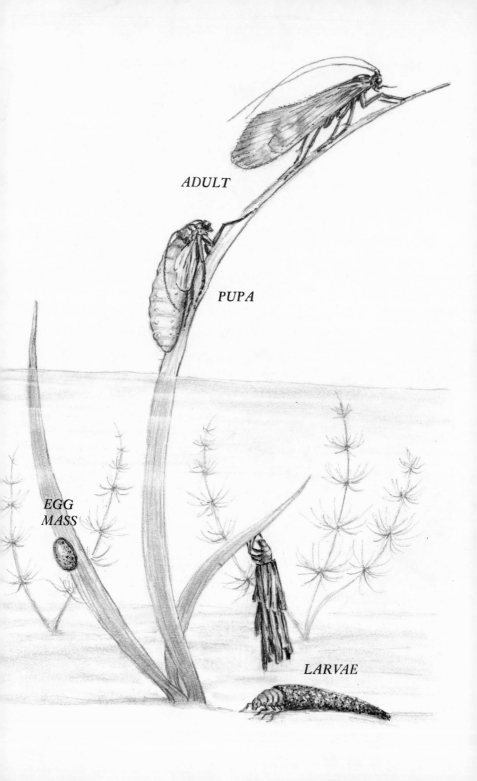

ADULT

PUPA

EGG
MASS

LARVAE

As water flows by, small animals and plants are swept into the open end of the funnel.

Meanwhile the caddis worm sits quietly in the narrow neck of the funnel. As food is washed in, the little larva dines at its leisure. Of course the trap net may become filled with sediment. But this is no great tragedy. The caddis worm simply moves out of this house and spins a new one.

Eventually the time comes when it must change over into an adult. Then the larva stops eating and seals up the door of its house. Inside the case it undergoes a series of wonderful changes. Just before the final change, it breaks out of its house and rises to the surface. There it locates a dry rock or twig and climbs aboard.

Soon the skin splits along its back and a crumpled caddis fly emerges. It sits for a while until its wings straighten and harden. Then it flutters away to spend its short life, and to help produce still another generation of caddis flies.

If you want to get better acquainted with the worms, look for the larvae among the pebbles in the shallow parts of ponds and streams. You may not recognize them at first. It is a strange sight to see a "dead" stick suddenly begin to crawl along the bottom.

When you finally do pick one up, you will find the larva inside, clinging tightly to the inner walls. It has a special pair of hooks at the far end of its abdomen that help it do this.

← *Life history of a caddis fly*

Since the caddis worm is soft and delicate, it had better be handled with care if you want it to stay alive. Perhaps you can pick the case apart very carefully. Can you spot the delicate strands of silk that bind the particles of building material together? Can you see the inside silk lining?

If you succeed in getting the caddis worm out in one piece, put it into a small aquarium (without fish), or into a glass jar, using pond water in either case. Now you can watch it build a new home. Try providing different kinds of building materials—sand, pebbles, bits of mica, fragments of toothpicks, pieces of cellophane or plastic. Will the caddis fly use any material you supply, or does it choose a particular kind?

Perhaps your caddis worm will build a house of clear cellophane fragments. In that case you could look right into the tube to see what it is doing.

Does the caddis worm prefer certain colors? Provide it with fragments of plastic or cellophane in a variety of colors. Does it use all the colors equally, or does it select some colors and ignore others?

7
Walk Into My Parlor

Once upon a time, in Greece, there lived a beautiful maiden named Arachne. She was a very skillful weaver, excelling all the other maidens of her time. Arachne wove magnificent cloths and tapestries. This great skill made her very conceited. In her vanity she dared to challenge Athena to a contest. Athena was the goddess of weaving.

Arachne soon discovered how foolish it was to challenge a goddess. According to the old Greek legends, Athena became so angry that she destroyed Arachne's exquisite tapestries. But even more than that, she changed the conceited girl into a spider and condemned her to a life of spinning.

Arachne became the Greek word for "spider." And modern biologists classify spiders as arachnids (together with scorpions, ticks, mites, and a few other related organisms). Legend aside, spiders are among the most artful spinners and weavers of the animal world. Their familiar webs are found everywhere—

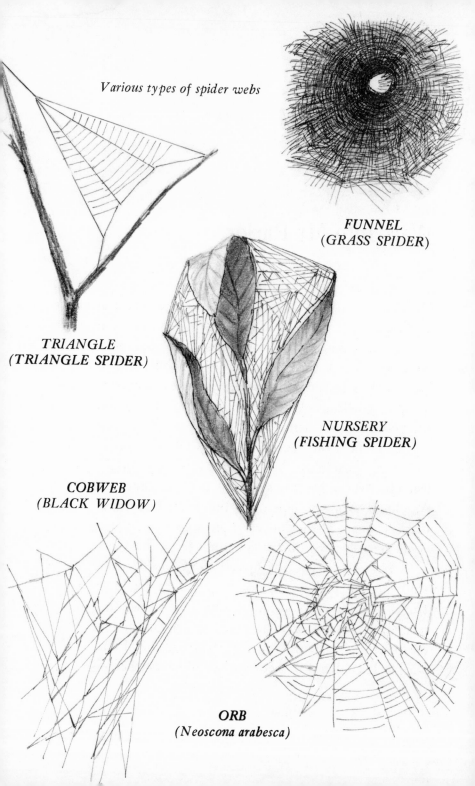

Various types of spider webs

FUNNEL
(GRASS SPIDER)

TRIANGLE
(TRIANGLE SPIDER)

NURSERY
(FISHING SPIDER)

COBWEB
(BLACK WIDOW)

ORB
(Neoscona arabesca)

in houses, basements, barns, gardens, back yards, fields, and forests.

Some webs are just a crazy hodge-podge of crossed threads. Others are beautiful creations with complex patterns that are artistically pleasing. Some are as closely woven as the finest silk sheets. They may hang like shimmering white curtains. Others are masterpieces of engineering—a silken dome, a wheel-like halo, a tunnel of silk slanting away from a horizontal platform. Of course, there are also many varieties of spiders that do not build any kind of web whatsoever.

To your mother, cobwebs up near the ceiling may be a sign of careless housekeeping. To you, it may be most annoying when you bump into trailing strands of silk as you are taking a stroll. You brush them away impatiently. But to the spider, those cobwebs and silken strands are life itself.

A spider uses its silk in many ways. One of these is to capture its prey. This use of the web has even been glamorized in a famous poem:

> "Will you walk into my parlour?" said
>   the spider to the fly;
> " 'Tis the prettiest little parlour that
>   ever you did spy."

The poem is quite accurate. The web is a pretty little parlor; and very effective too. The spider is a master trapper, and since this book is about trappers, Arachne deserves a place of honor. So let us begin with the building of the silken trap.

The spider has a soft, plump abdomen containing a large number of special silk-producing glands. The silk is drawn out of the body through a number of nozzle-like openings (spinnerets) at the rear end of the abdomen. The silk comes out as a liquid which hardens into a strand as it hits the air.

The silk must be pulled out of the spinnerets. Sometimes the spider fastens one end of the strand to a twig and drops away. The farther away the spider moves, the longer the strand of silk becomes. At other times the spider uses a hind leg to pull the silk out. When it has pulled out as much as it wants, it reaches back and cuts the strand with a claw on the tip of its foot. Sometimes the animal releases a length of silken thread into the wind. The force of the breeze is enough to pull many feet of silk out of its abdomen.

Each kind of spider builds a trap of its own special design. How does it learn to do this? Most spiders die in the fall, leaving behind an egg case full of eggs to produce the next generation. The young spiders emerge in the spring. By this time the old web has long been destroyed.

The young spider never saw her mother's web. She never got a lesson in web-building from the parents she never met. She never watched any other spider construct a trap. She never saw a spider capture a fly, wrap the fly in a silken mummy case and haul it off.

And yet she seems to know just how to do these things. How does she know? Biologists say it is instinct, but this does not mean very much. "Instinct" in simply a word that covers up an unsolved mystery. So let us admit that we really don't know how a spider learns to build its special kind of trap. But we must admit that trap-building in the spider is a remarkable adaptation for staying alive. And, even though we do not understand how the spider learns to build its web, this should not stop us from watching her do it.

The colorful garden spider belongs to a group called the orb-weavers. All the spiders of this group build remarkable wheel-shaped webs. Some of their traps are several feet across. Others are small. It all depends on the size of the spider and the location in which it is working. Let us watch the complicated engineering that goes into the building of an orb web.

The garden spider stands on a twig with the rear end of its abdomen raised in the air. It pulls a silken thread out of a spinneret and releases it. The thread is so light that it is carried off on the slightest breeze, growing longer and longer as it floats away.

Often the floating strand spins out into empty space. What a waste of silk! But the spider does not give up. It simply gets rid of the wasted thread and sends out a new one. The action is repeated over and over again until the floating strand finally catches onto another twig. When the far end is secure, the spider cuts off the silk near its abdomen and anchors it to the twig on which it is standing. When the thread is attached at both ends, it forms the first bridge of the web.

The spider runs across the bridge, adding more threads to strengthen it. It drops downward from the bridge and attaches additional threads to other twigs. Finally a foundation is built in the form of a roughly rectangular frame. Now it spins a new thread across the frame. It walks out on this thread to the middle. After attaching a new thread there, it rushes back to the outside of the frame.

It makes many trips between the outside of the frame and the middle point, adding thread after thread. These strands resemble the spokes of a wheel, or the radii of a circle. Each time the spider pauses at the center it adds threads that tie the spokes together. Pretty soon it has built the middle of the web into a cushion large enough to sit upon.

Now the busy animal lays down a spiral of silk beginning from the cushion in the center and working outward. It goes around and around, from spoke to spoke, fastening the silk at each point. This spiral will be her guide line for the final step in web-making.

Up to this point the threads were made of dry silk. They were not at all sticky, so they could hardly serve to catch insects. Now the spider lays down a

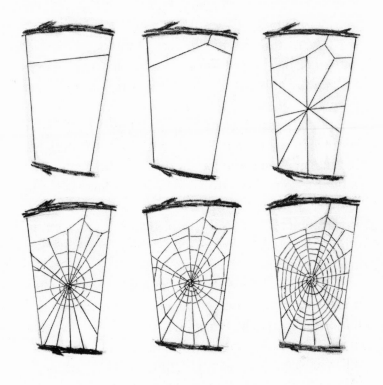

Steps in the building of an orb web. The methods vary. In some cases the spider will let a breeze carry the first thread across between two twigs; in others it will walk from one twig to the tree or ground and back along the other twig, carrying the silk line. Once the initial "bridgehead" is set up, making a successful web is a matter of work and inherited skills. It drops with gravity, walks across, walks up or down, and measures, always spinning out more silk, which it fastens at the intersections. The spider begins the spiral at the center but soon reverses itself and lays it from the outside to the hub, rolling up the temporary spiral as it goes.

new spiral of sticky threads. This time it begins at the outside. It works its way from spoke to spoke, moving inward towards the center. It walks on the old, dry guide spiral as it works. With each step it bites off and discards the old dry threads that it no longer needs.

Finally it adds some zig-zag ribbons or silk above and below the center. At last it is ready for business. It takes its place on the cushion in the center and waits for something to happen. If the lines begin to vibrate, it indicates that a victim has been trapped. It runs quickly across the trap. If the victim is struggling, the spider throws layers and layers of silk around it until the insect is bound up like a mummy.

Now the spider can set the morsel aside. When it is ready for the feast, it pounces on the mummified bundle and sinks its fangs into the prey. A few tiny drops of poison are injected, which kill the victim. Then it sucks all the body fluids out of the prey. When all the nutriment has been sucked out, the remains are cut loose and dropped out of the web. It makes a few repairs in the trap and sits back until the next victim is caught.

Spider silk is an amazing substance. It seems fragile and delicate, yet a strand of this silk is actually stronger and more elastic than a filament of steel of the same thickness. Besides, spiders can produce many different kinds of silks at will. There is dry silk and sticky silk; silk that solidifies into strands and silk that forms gluelike droplets; silk that comes out as a single thread and silk that comes out in ribbon-like bands. There seems to be a special silk for every need.

Here are some of the uses that a spider makes of the various kinds of silks:

1. Dragline, or rope on which to swing or go up and down.
2. Home or lair in which to live and hide.
3. Trap or web in which to capture prey.
4. Trapline with which to manipulate the trap.
5. "Telegraphic" alarm system to notify the spider when the trap has visitors.
6. Swaddling cloth with which to bind victims.
7. Banquet hall in which to feast on the prey.
8. "Marriage bed" on which male and female can mate.
9. Tough protective cocoon for eggs.
10. Aerial balloon for free-floating trips through the air.

The spider has not been the only user of spider silk. Man is an ingenious creature who often steals the products of other animals if he finds them to be useful, and spider silk is certainly inviting. In ancient times the native peoples of New Guinea, the Solomon Islands, and South America used spider silks for fishing. In some cases they made kites of leaves and sailed them over the water, trailing strands of spider silk. As the silk dragged through the water, fish got entangled in the strands, and thus they were trapped.

More recently there were attempts to use spider silk to make fabrics. For example, in 1709 an industrious Frenchman actually manufactured stockings and gloves out of spider silk. Unfortunately for him, spider silk could not compete with that of the silkworm. The silkworm is much easier to handle and it produces a good deal more silk.

Nevertheless, spider silk was used in optical instruments until a few decades ago. The notorious black widow spider was one of the best producers of this commercial spider silk. Another excellent silk producer was the harmless banded garden spider. Female spiders were used because they are usually larger than males and produce more silk. The spiders were raised in glass jars and fed on flies, gnats, crickets, and other insects.

When a spider was to be "silked," she was placed on her back on a soft piece of wood. The operator fastened her down by putting a staple over her narrow waist. Additional staples were driven in to hold her legs spread out. The operator had to be careful not to injure her, because he wanted to use the same spider many times. A healthy, uninjured female spider could be silked more than twenty times. And each time she produced about 100 feet or more of valuable silk.

With the spider in position, the operator pulled

silk out of her abdomen through a spinneret. As he pulled it out, he wound it up in spiral form on a U-shaped frame. The dragline type of silk was generally used, because it is probably the strongest silk a spider produces. It is dry, without sticky globules attached. It is not affected by changes in temperature or humidity, and when stretched across a metal ring it remained straight and true. That is why spider silk was, until recently, the ideal choice for the cross hairs in gunsights, range finders, transits, telescopes, and other optical instruments. Today the necessary lines are made by being etched on glass or by using extremely fine wires.

Of course, spiders come in two sexes. In many species the males may be only half the size of the females. But in other species, males and females are equal. Often it is hard to identify a male until he is sexually mature. There is a story about a spider expert who had a pet tarantula named Isabella. Suddenly he discovered that he had to change the name to Ferdinand.

How did he know? When a male spider is ready for mating, he develops a pair of enlarged bulbs near his head. Any time you meet a spider that seems to be wearing boxing gloves, you can be sure that he is an adult male. He spins a small, flat web on which he deposits a drop or two of fluid loaded with male reproductive cells (sperms). Then he turns around and fills those bulbs at his head with the sperm-laden

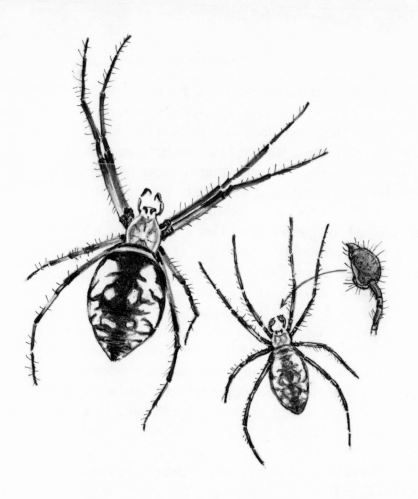

The orange garden spider Argiope aurantia, *the female at left, the male at right. The hairy palps of the male, one of which is shown enlarged, identify its sex unquestionably.*

fluid. At last he is ready to hunt for a mate, but there are certain problems.

In many ways spiders are strange creatures. The females are very independent, and often they don't care for company. Males that approach may be in danger of being killed and eaten. Therefore the male must be very cautious. Before approaching the female, he must discover what her intentions might be. He uses special signals to notify the female that he is a hopeful mate rather than a meal.

The male garden spider does this in an interesting way. He builds a bridge to the edge of the female's web in the form of a strong thread of silk. Then he retreats to the far end of his bridge. From the safety of this position he vibrates the web in a special way. The female recognizes the signal. If she is ready to mate, she hurries to meet him by rushing across the "bridge of love."

Other spiders use different signals. Perhaps the male stands with his legs held out in a way that the female cannot resist. Perhaps he taps her leg very carefully with one of his own. Perhaps he brings her a present of food; then with her mouth full she is unable to attack him. In any case he is ready to leave in a hurry if the female shows that she is about to attack.

If the female is ready to mate, the male transfers his sperms to the reproductive opening beneath her abdomen. Then he runs for his life. He may be lucky enough to get away, or he may be eaten on the spot. Meanwhile the eggs are fertilized inside the female's body.

The female lays hundreds of fertilized eggs. She protects them by spinning a silken egg case or cocoon.

She hangs the cocoon in her web or in some other protected place. In some species the female attaches the cocoon to her own body and drags it along wherever she goes.

Eggs that are laid in the fall hatch rather quickly. But the young spiders spend the winter inside the cocoon. In the spring the spiderlings come out. All they have to do is eat and grow into mature adult spiders.

Sometimes the young spiders go on a long trip. They climb to some high point, face into the wind, and spin out a delicate thread. When the pull becomes strong enough, the little spiders are carried off on their silken parachutes. Ships at sea, many miles from land, have reported seeing such small aeronauts floating about—a remarkable adaptation for finding new homes.

Now that you know so much about spiders, perhaps you will look at them and their webs with different eyes. Have you ever seen an orb web in the early morning when it is glistening with drops of dew? You can make a permanent record of this beauty with a camera. Spider-web photography is a fascinating hobby that challenges the skill and ingenuity of the most ardent picture-taker.

The spider's trap is practically invisible most of the time. And if it is invisible to the eye, it is also invisible to the camera lens. But if you catch it when it is glistening with dew, it shines in all its beauty.

A wet orb web seems to be made of many strands of seed pearls.

Some web photographers carry a small spray bottle to create artificial dew. When they find a suitable spider web, they apply a fine spray of droplets. It is best to set the diaphragm at its smallest opening and to get as close up as the camera will allow. A tripod-mounted camera will give a steadier picture than a hand-held camera. It also helps if the web is backlighted or sidelighted.

If you find an abandoned web, test the strands for stickiness. Touch one of the spokes of the wheel very gently with the tip of a pencil. Does it stick to the pencil as you pull away? Now touch a thread of the circling spiral. Does it stick? Explore various parts of the web in this way. Which parts are sticky and which parts are dry?

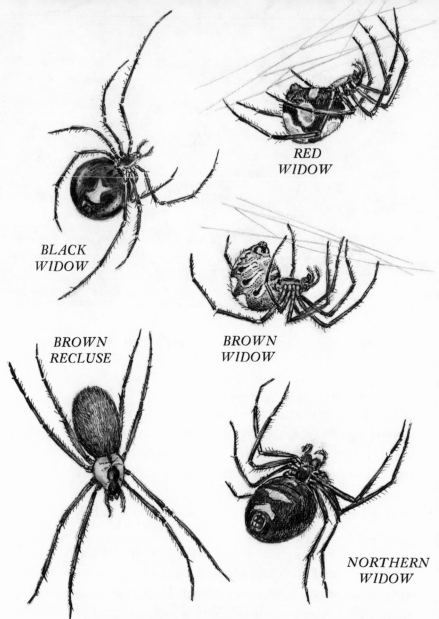

RED
WIDOW

BLACK
WIDOW

BROWN
RECLUSE

BROWN
WIDOW

NORTHERN
WIDOW

Most people have heard of only one poisonous spider, the black widow, but all of these inject poison. The brown widow, which is found on or near buildings, is less toxic than the black. The red markings on the abdomens of the northern and black widow may resemble an hourglass, but they vary in shape. The beautifully spotted red widow is found only in Florida—so far. The brown recluse lives in houses, generally on the floor, behind furniture, or in cloth. All those shown are females.

Perhaps you would prefer to deal with a spider itself, rather than with the web. If you are going to work with spiders, you must learn to recognize the harmful varieties. Leave the study of dangerous spiders to spider experts. There are plenty of harmless spiders to work with.

Would you like to watch a spider build its trap while you relax in the comfort of your home? You can. Just capture a harmless spider and put it into a large jar with a cover. The spider will soon begin to spin while you can watch with a hand lens. If the spider does not begin to work as quickly as you would like, put in a twig and a couple of dry curled-up leaves. This may stimulate it into getting to work. After the web is completed, feed its owner small insects. Occasionally put a very few drops of water into the jar.

It is easy to collect lots of small insects for spider food. Simply sweep the grass with an insect net. Throw a couple of the captured insects into the web. How does the spider react? How does it mummify the victims with silk? Does it feast on the victims wherever they are caught in the web? Or does it prefer a particular part of the web for eating?

Toward fall you can often find a spider web with egg cases or cocoons attached. These cocoons can provide many interesting research opportunities. How many eggs does a cocoon contain? How long will it be before the young spiders hatch? Does the mother guard the cocoon? Does she care for the young after they hatch? Are there any parasites in the cocoon that destroy the young spiders?

Suspend a cocoon in a covered jar and wait for developments. You may be surprised to see how many young spiders hatch out of a single cocoon. Do these newly hatched spiders build webs? Don't be surprised if you see young spiders attack and eat their brothers and sisters. This is perfectly normal spider behavior.

Once you have learned to handle these arachnids, you can demonstrate the production of silk. You must hold the spider with its underside up. Then touch the spinneret with the tip of a toothpick or the wrong end of a thin paintbrush. When the silk sticks, start moving the toothpick slowly away from the spider. A thread of silk will develop right before your eyes.

If you let an assistant pull the stick farther and farther away, the silk thread will become longer and longer. Watch through a hand lens meanwhile—you can see the silk streaming out of the spinneret. Try wrapping the silk on a frame as the commercial producers do.

8
The Sparkling Dewdrop Trap

James Thurber once wrote a book called *Fables for Our Time*. One of these fables deals with the adventures of a "fairly intelligent fly."

A large spider built a web in which to trap flies. This spider had already captured hundreds of flies, so she was quite experienced in the trapping business. As soon as a fly was caught in the web, she pounced on it, ate it quickly, and got rid of the remains. Thus she kept her web spic and span, so that the flies of the neighborhood wouldn't realize it was a trap.

One day the fairly intelligent fly came along. The spider waited patiently for the fly to land on her nice clean web, but the fly just kept buzzing around. Finally the spider got tired of waiting. She came out of her hiding place and said very politely to the fly, "Come into my parlor," or words to that effect. But the fairly intelligent fly explained that he never landed unless he saw other flies. "And," said he, "I don't see any other flies in your parlor, so I'm leaving."

A little later he came to a place where he saw many other flies dancing about. In spite of a friendly warning from a passing bee, the fly zoomed over to join the dancing. No sooner did he settle down than he was stuck in the mucilage on a sheet of flypaper.

Mr. Thurber concluded that "there is no safety in numbers, or in anything else." But we are going to draw a slightly different conclusion. We would say to the fly, "If a spider's trap won't get you, then an innocent-looking mucilage trap will."

Who do you think invented flypaper? If you say it was man, you are wrong. Long before people even existed on earth, certain plants were already producing mucilage-covered insect traps. These plants can certainly be classed as trappers because they capture insects and use them for food. They are called by various names.

One insect-trapping plant that grows in Spain and Portugal is known locally as "the flycatcher." The native people hang branches of it in their houses as a sort of flypaper. The surface of its leaves is covered with countless glands that produce droplets of clear mucilage. These droplets make the leaves sparkle in the sun as though they were covered with dewdrops.

Any insect that lands on the innocent-looking leaves is trapped. Lumps of the gummy stuff stick to its legs, its wings, its body. The insect tries to crawl

A butterwort, Pinguicula

out, but its legs get heavier and heavier as more mucilage hangs on. Finally, the insect sinks down and dies.

The glands on the leaf secrete digestive fluids in
addition to the mucilage. These fluids slowly change
the proteins of the insect's body. The digested nutrients find their way into the cells of the plant.

Butterwort is another plant that uses mucilage-
covered leaves which trap insects. This plant grows
in swampy places of the northern half of our earth.
The plant produces a cluster of leaves close to the
ground. The edges of each leaf curl slightly, as you see
in the picture. Thus the leaf resembles a shallow

saucer. The leaf surface is covered with two kinds of glands—those that produce "fly glue" and those that produce digestive fluids.

The story is the same. If a gnat or other tiny insect lands on the butterwort leaf, it is soon trapped in sticky mucilage. The more the insect struggles, the more glue oozes out to cover it. Eventually the insect dies and is digested.

There is a very interesting sidelight concerning butterwort. Years ago, farm folk used butterwort leaves to cover open wounds on their cattle. They believed that it had antiseptic qualities and hastened healing. Interestingly enough, some modern biologists believe that the leaves of butterwort give off some kind of antibiotic, a bacteria-killing substance.

Of all the "flypaper" plants, perhaps the most interesting is the sundew. It has small, circular leaves that are covered with tentacles. Wouldn't you agree that tentacles on a plant are a most unusual adaptation? The sundew is a small plant that lives in bogs and swamps in many parts of the world. Each plant forms a small rosette of leaves near the ground. These leaves are covered with prominent glandular hairs that stand up straight. Each of these bristle-like hairs has a clear bubble of sticky mucilage on its tip. When the rays of the sun strike the clear drops on the tips of the tentacles, they gleam and glisten like drops of dew.

When an insect touches one of the sticky drops, it becomes entangled in the mucilage. As the insect

The sundew, Drosera, showing the hairs tipped with mucilage

tries to free itself, it touches other hairs. And now a most amazing thing begins to happen. One after another, the glandular hairs begin to bend toward the victim, like the tentacles of an octopus. Soon many tentacles are curled about the victim. The prey is buried in sticky glue and pressed down towards the surface of the leaf. The trapper has captured its prey.

When digestion is completed, there is nothing left of the insect except its indigestible skeleton. Then the tentacles open up again and the remains blow away in the wind, or are washed away by the next rain. Meanwhile the useful end-products of digestion are taken into the cells of the leaf.

There are quite a number of ways in which certain plants can move. One of the most remarkable is the movement of a sundew's hairs toward a trapped insect, gluing it down firmly without any chance of escape.

The sundew is such an unusual plant that it has aroused the curiosity of many people. Among them was the famous English biologist named Charles Darwin. He is best known for his theory of evolution by natural selection, but somehow he found time in his busy life to experiment with sundews.

His interest in the sundew began in 1860 during a vacation. He noticed that these innocent-looking plants were trapping lots of insects. He wrote, "I carried home some plants, and on giving them insects, saw the movement of the tentacles. This made me think it probable that the insects were caught for some special purpose."

After many experiments, he concluded that this special function of the plants was obtaining food. The sundews were actually digesting the insects and using the digested nutrients. At one time Darwin remarked to a friend, "By Jove, I sometimes think the sundew is a disguised animal!"

Perhaps you can repeat some of the tests that Darwin made. For example, how do the tentacles of a sundew plant react if you give them a live insect? A tiny fragment of meat? A speck of fish? A fiber of gelatin? A sliver of wood? A grain of sand? A particle of plastic? A snip of plant material? A crumb of bread? A bit of cheese?

If you try any of these things, remember this: the portion you serve to the sundew must be very small indeed. If you think your offering is small enough, divide it in half and you will probably be closer to the right size.

When Darwin described his experiments, some biologists refused to accept his conclusions. They were unable to bring themselves to believe that a plant could digest insects for food. They said that Darwin did not actually prove that the sundew made use of any part of the trapped insects.

Darwin's son Francis answered the criticism with an experiment. He collected a large number of sundews and divided them into two groups. Both groups were raised under exactly the same conditions. However, one group was fed meat, while the other group remained unfed. Here is the conclusion of the experiment as stated by Francis Darwin.

"On the fed side the leaves are much larger, differently colored, and more numerous; flower stalks are taller and more numerous; and I believe there are far more seed capsules."

This is another experiment that you can repeat if you like. However, let us give you one word of caution: *in many states the sundew is protected by law*. So don't try to bring sundew plants home.

You might be able to do some experiments out in the field where the sundews live. Or perhaps you can work out an arrangement with the local botanic garden, if your community has one. However, to work at home, you will have to buy some plants from a licensed dealer.

9
The Stinging-Cell Trap

Around 1740, a Swiss biologist, Abraham Trembley, fished some green water weeds out of a ditch. Under his microscope he saw many strange animals hanging onto them. Perhaps the queerest of all was a tiny tube-like creature with a circle of long, coiling tentacles at one end. The animal was so small that he could hardly see it with his naked eye. Yet it lived, and ate, and reproduced.

Trembley was so intrigued with this strange creature that he began a series of experiments. In one, he "killed" the animal by cutting off its head. Much to his surprise, the animal did not die. In a few days it had grown a new head and went about its business as though nothing had happened. Then Trembley discovered that by making his cuts in a special way, he could force the animal to grow several heads.

These experiments reminded Trembley of an ancient Greek myth. Perhaps you remember the story of Hercules. He was assigned the task of destroying the hydra, a monstrous sea serpent with nine heads. Each time Hercules lopped off one head with his sharp sword, two new heads grew in its place. So Trembley called his animal a hydra.

The hydra is a trapper. It lives by capturing and eating small animals that swim about it in the water. If you want to picture a hydra, think of a small piece of string, perhaps half to three-quarters of an inch long. It is generally attached by one end to a leaf of a water plant. The other end hangs free. This free end is raveled into separate threads—usually six—that spread in various directions.

The body of a hydra is a hollow tube. It has an attachment point at one end, sometimes called the foot. At the other end is a mouth surrounded by a cluster of tentacles. The tentacles are long, delicate, sensitive structures floating freely in the water. They can twist and coil like a worm or a snake.

The hydra's body is very elastic. It can stretch to its full length of an inch or more when the hydra is relaxed. Or, if disturbed, it can contract to an almost invisible bump on the leaf to which it is attached. When it is contracted, you would find it hard to recognize it as a hydra.

The tentacles are most elastic of all. When they are pulled in they become stubby bumps on the hydra's body. But at other times they can become longer then the total body length. When this happens the tentacles become so incredibly thin and trans-

A hydra, with a new hydra budding off at the right. The rounded mass on its left side is an ovum, an egg ready to be fertilized and develop into a new hydra. These animals are unusual in their ability to reproduce in two different ways, sometimes at the same time. The bulge in the upper part, near the tantacles, is from a water flea that is being digested.

parent that they are nearly invisible threads in the water. A close look at the tentacles shows that they are covered with bumps over their entire length. Each bump is a battery of stinging cells called nematocysts that are used in the capture of prey.

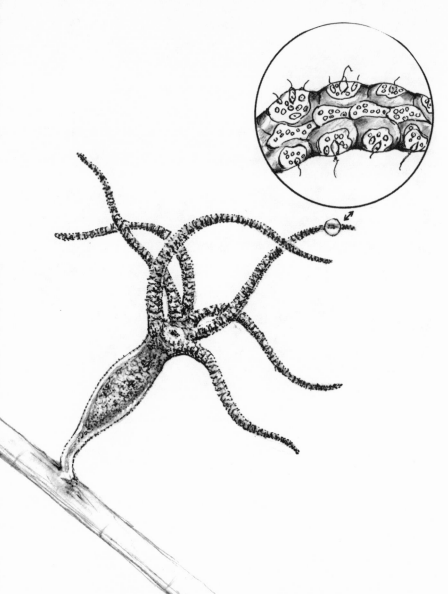

The hydra's tentacles are formidable trapping machines. In the circle is a close-up showing the stinging cells.

A hydra never goes hunting for victims. It depends on its ability as a trapper. It hangs quietly from a leaf, a twig, or even the surface film of the water. In this relaxed position its tentacles trail out in every direction. They are so delicate, yet those tentacles are a deadly trap for any small worm or water flea that may come along. Some of the larger hydras can trap even newly hatched fish.

Picture a water flea progressing through the water. It darts this way and that in a jerky course. By chance it brushes one of those trailing tentacles. Battery after battery of stinging cells is discharged by the tentacle. Each battery discharges several different

A daphnia, one of several small animals commonly called water fleas, being trapped by a hydra. Some of the stinging cells shoot out gluey threads, as shown here, and additional tentacles may move in to aid capture.

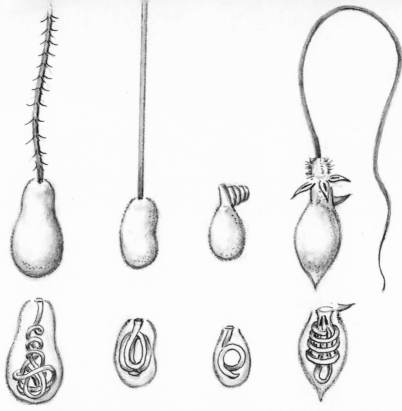

Four kinds of nematocysts of a hydra, shown undischarged at bottom, discharged at top. The two types on the left are glutinant, or sticky. Third from left is volvent, a thread that wraps around parts of the prey like the bola, a lariat with stone weights on the end. The type at the right contains large barbs that enter the prey and shoot a poison into it. Each of these elaborate mechanisms is produced by a single body cell.

kinds of weapons. Some of them are springlike coils that wrap around the legs and bristles of the victim. Others are long threads coated with a glue that fastens to the victim's body. But the most unusual ones are like tiny harpoons. They actually penetrate the tissues of the victim. These little darts are built like hollow hypodermic needles. As they enter the body of the prey, they inject a posionous fluid that serves as an anesthetic.

If there is any difficulty in overcoming the trapped victim, other tentacles bend over and hold it. The prey may struggle for a bit, but it cannot get away. Soon the anesthetic takes effect and the creature quiets down. Now the tentacles carry the food toward the mouth. The mouth opens, the victim is stuffed into the hydra's hollow body, and the mouth closes again. Digestion begins immediately. The tentacles are extended once again. The trap is set for another victim.

Hydras make fine pets of a sort if you take the trouble to learn how to keep them. They can live comfortably in a wine glass or baby-food jar. All you have to do is feed them on schedule, and change the water in which they live. If you go on vacation, simply cover the jar in which they live and store them in the refrigerator (not in the freezer, however). They'll be there waiting for you when you come back.

They come in a variety of colors—brown, gray, white, green. You can buy any of these species in living cultures from a biological-supply company. They usually send along instructions for feeding them and keeping them alive and well. If you buy hydras, you might as well get the brown ones. They are the largest, the sturdiest, and the easiest ones for beginners to raise.

On the other hand, you may want the pleasure of

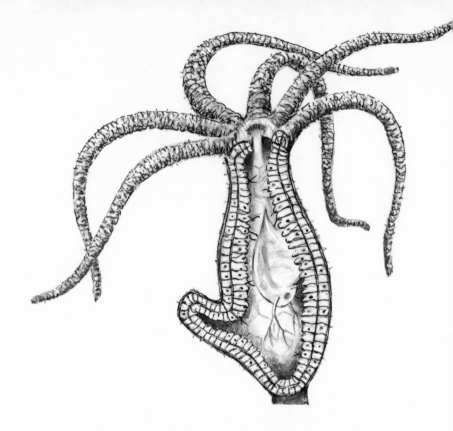

Cross section of a hydra showing the two layers of cells it is made of, with a layer of jelly-like material between the layers. Some of the interior cells give out digestive juices that will turn the daphnia into fragments, which will then be digested by other interior cells.

taking a field trip to find your own hydras. But you will have to accept whatever kinds you may find. Hydras usually cling to the water plants growing in ponds, pools, springs, or streams. Fish up some submerged weeds and put them into a large jar of water from the same source. Be sure to include some decaying material from the bottom of the pond. To increase your chances of getting hydras, collect several jars of material from different areas.

Even if you have captured some hydras you won't see them immediately. Remember, when they are disturbed they contract down to tiny blobs that are hardly noticed. Take the jars home and let them stand undisturbed for a while; then examine them against the light of a window. If you were lucky enough to get a few hydras, they will be relaxed, and stretched to full size. You will see them clinging to the plants, to the sides of the jar, or even to the water film at the top.

The hydra may be small, but it has a big appetite. However, it eats only living food. It will eat live worms and water fleas by the dozen, but dead water fleas or dead worms have no attraction. This may create a problem, because you must always have a supply of living victims to feed your pets.

If you have a pond or lake nearby from which you can collect water fleas like Daphnia or Cyclops, you are in luck. Otherwise you may have to buy tubifex worms from an aquarium-supply store. Most biologists who raise hydras today feed them on brine shrimps. Brine shrimp eggs are available from any aquarium-supply store. They hatch quickly in salt water, and hydras thrive on them.

However, salt water kills hydras, so you can't pour the newly hatched brine shrimps right into your hydra cultures. You must first wash away the salt.

Pour the newly hatched brine shrimps into a fine net. You can even use a clean handkerchief poked through a ring made by your thumb and forefinger. After the salt water runs through, pour clean pond water over the shrimps which are left in the net. Then drop them into the hydra culture.

After allowing the hydras to feed for a half-hour or so, get rid of all the dead and dying shrimps that remain. If you leave them in the jar, they will foul the culture and the hydras will die. Simply empty the glass with the culture into another container. Most of the hydras will stick to the glass, so they won't be poured out. Refill the jar immediately with fresh pond water, and the hydras will thrive until the next feeding.

Never add tap water to your hydra cultures. Tap water is toxic to the animals. You can use aquarium water from an established tank, or bottled spring water, or clear water that you get from a pond, stream, or well. You will find more detailed information on the care and culturing of hydras in *Experiments with Microscopic Animals*, in the Suggested Reading list.

If you feed your hydras regularly, and give them care, they will grow and reproduce. You can tell that they are reproducing when you see small hydras budding right out of the sides of the parents. Eventually the buds break away and become adults. From time to time, take a census of the number of hydras in your jar. You can then plot a graph to show their population growth.

Try cutting a hydra into two or more pieces. It is not easy, and yet you can do it if you practice. If you succeed, put each piece in a separate dish of pond water. Keep the dishes covered so the water does not dry out and watch for developments. You may be surprised at the result.

Hydra-watching is easy and interesting. How does a hydra move from place to place? Can a hydra swim? Do you find any dead ones in your culture? How do the hydras react to a bright light shining on one side of their home? Do they move toward the light, away from it, or don't they seem to care? What happens if you rap the table sharply, close to the culture? What does a hydra do if you touch it with the tip of a needle? If you drop a fragment of raw meat into its tentacles?

Most interesting of all is to watch a hydra capture its prey. What amazing adaptations those delicate tentacles with their batteries of stinging cells are. You can see these nematocysts under a microscope. Put

One of the oddest things you may be able to observe is a hydra moving about by somersaulting.

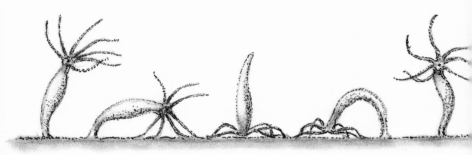

a hydra on a slide under a microscope and see if you can make it discharge them. Does a 5 per cent solution of ordinary table salt do the trick? Will other household chemicals work? Try sugar, milk, Epsom salts, bicarbonate of soda, food coloring. How many different types of stingers does your hydra release?

If you want to see a real struggle, put a single healthy hydra into a small dish of pond water and add a single lively tubifex worm. The worm is three or four times as long as the hydra. You will witness quite a battle.

10
Faster Than the Eye Can See

Imagine a mousetrap that sets itself automatically. Once it was set, any mouse that approached would be promptly sucked into the trap. Next the self-acting trap would destroy the mouse and reset itself so that it was ready for another.

Such a trap is already in existence; you don't have to invent it. A lowly plant did it first.

The plant is called the utricularia. Its underwater leaves are covered with miniature traps that function automatically. The traps look like tiny sacs or bladders. Therefore the plant is commonly known as bladderwort.

Bladderworts are found all over the world. They come in many varieties. Most of them are water plants living in quiet ponds, bogs, or slow-moving streams. The illustration shows the arrangement of parts in a common variety that lives in the United States.

The bladders capture various small creatures that live in the water. Their victims include protozoa, water fleas, worms, insect larvae, and even newly

The traps of a utricularia, or bladderwort, enlarged

hatched fish. Bladderworts are expert trappers. Let us use our imaginations a little, so we can learn something about their amazingly efficient traps.

We are watching a little water flea (Daphnia or Cyclops) darting about in our aquarium. In its wanderings the daphnid approaches a bladderwort plant floating quietly in the water. It swims closer, and closer.... Suddenly it disappears before our eyes. How could it disappear so suddenly that the eye couldn't follow? If you look really close, perhaps with a magnifying glass, you can solve the mystery. The water flea is inside one of the bladders of the bladderwort. The plant didn't seem to do anything at all. And yet it captured the water flea.

The truth of the matter is this: bladderwort traps work faster than the human eye can see. For years biologists who studied the bladders could not figure out exactly what happened. They failed because they depended on their eyes, and their eyes just couldn't see fast enough. Even a microscope failed to help.

However, a British biologist named Francis E. Lloyd finally used high-speed movies to solve the mystery. He took pictures at intervals of a hundredth of a second. After studying many sequences of high-speed pictures, he found the answer.

Each bladder is a tiny oval or pear-shaped sac, with an entrance at one side. The entrance is guarded by a double flap of tissue set back in a shallow recess or hallway. The outer flap is the door. It is attached at the top edge, but the lower part hangs free like a

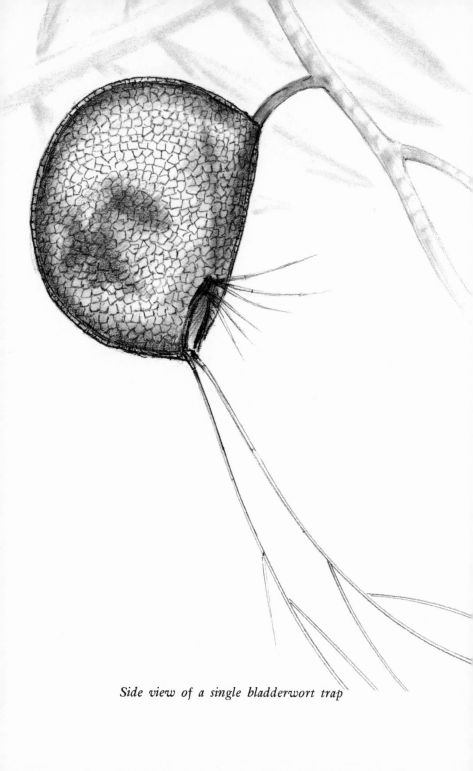

Side view of a single bladderwort trap

curtain. The free end of the curtain-door cannot swing out of the recess in which it hangs. It is prevented from doing this by a collar of cells at the bottom. Thus, the curtain-door can open only inward, *into* the sac.

The inner flap presses against the curtain-door and the cell-collar from the inside. Together the two flaps make an effective seal. In addition, the collar is covered with gland cells. These glands produce a sticky mucilage that cements the flaps to the collar. The double flap plus the mucilage taken together make the door completely watertight. Water can neither enter the bladder nor leave when these flaps are closed.

The entrance is surrounded by a cluster of branching, bristle-like hairs. Imagine that these hairs form the slanting sides of a funnel, with the door at the bottom. The funnel of bristles serves to guide small creatures inward, towards the trap entrance.

The guide-bristles are *not* attached to the door, but to the tissue around it. However, there are two other pairs of stiff bristles attached to the bottom of the curtain-door. They are the triggers that open the door.

Before the trap can work, it must be set. This is done automatically in a very special way. High-speed movies show that water is drawn out of the bladder. We are not exactly sure how the water is withdrawn. However, clusters of four-armed hairs lining the inside of the sac seem to be involved in some way. We do know that it is a matter of pressure. At first the pres-

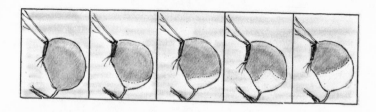

A bladderwort trap setting itself, drawn after a slow-motion movie film. At left the trap is full of water. In the next four pictures the water is gradually removed. When the trap is fully set, about 88 per cent of the water has gone out of it. Modified from Lloyd's The Carnivorous Plants.

sure inside and outside the sac are exactly equal. As water is withdrawn, the pressure inside the trap drops lower and lower. Water cannot rush in from the outside because the door is sealed.

The situation becomes very unbalanced and delicate. A low, negative pressure develops inside the trap, while the pressure outside remains as high as it was before. The smallest opening in the trap would cause water to come rushing into the sac under great force.

When the trap is in this unbalanced condition it is set and ready for action. It is ready to capture any unsuspecting daphnid that comes along. Like a vacuum cleaner with a clogged nozzle, it is not picking up anything at the moment. But once the nozzle is cleared, anything nearby is sucked in. A medicine dropper works in more or less the same way as the bladderwort trap.

The water flea hits the guide bristles and is directed inward. Down the funnel it goes toward the

A bladderwort trap works something like a medicine drop-per. At left the dropper is full of water, and the water pressure inside it is equal to the pressure outside it. When the water is squeezed out by compressing the air in the bulb, the water outside has a higher pressure and pushes back in as soon as the bulb is released, taking the daphnia in with it.

trigger hairs. The daphnid bumps one of the triggers, but the stiff hair does not bend. It acts like a straight lever that pushes the bottom of the curtain-door ever so slightly. But this slight push is enough to break the seal at the collar.

It is only a tiny break, but it is enough. The vacuum cleaner goes into action. Water from the out-side rushes into the bladder under pressure. It swings the curtain-door open for a fraction of a second. The victim is swept into the trap. The door closes again.

Once the door closes, the trap begins to reset it-self. It takes a little while for the water that rushed in to be withdrawn. Meanwhile the captive daphnid disintegrates. Soon only the "bones" of the victim remain to tell the story. We are not sure what causes the little prey animal to break down. Is it some digestive fluid produced by the cells of the bladder? Is it by the action of decay bacteria? Whatever the cause, the bladderwort plant benefits by absorbing some of the released nutrients.

Bladderworts often catch worms that are longer than the trap. The door slams shut with part of the worm inside the bladder and part outside. The curtain-like door flap squeezes hard against the soft body of the worm and hugs it tight. If the worm can break at the point where it is held, the part outside the trap escapes and may live. Otherwise a little more of the worm is sucked into the trap, then a little more, until the whole worm is engulfed.

These bladders catch one-called plants and animals, worms, water fleas, insect larvae, and other small creatures. But fish? It is hard to think that a quiet floating plant, without the power of movement, can catch a fast-moving creature like a fish. Yet there is no doubt that bladderworts can do it.

This surprising discovery was made in 1884 by a British observer named G. E. Simms, Jr. The illustration shows what another man observed in 1885. Since then many biologists from all parts of the world have seen bladderworts with young fish entangled in their traps. Perhaps you can see it too.

Bladderworts can be collected in many ponds, bogs, or streams. Take a few sprigs home and put them into an aquarium. This is a free-floating plant, so you don't have to root it. When the bladderwort is established in your tank, you may be able to see the traps in action. Don't get impatient. It takes lots of patience and keen observation.

What can you feed them? Every aquarium-supply store sells small living animals for fish food, such as Daphnia, Cyclops, or tubifex worms. Any one of these can be used to test the trapping powers of your bladderwort. You can also buy your living materials from a biological-supply house. They will probably be more expensive. But they carry a much wider variety of living cultures, including worms such as planaria, aelosoma, dero, enchytraeus, redworms, and others.

Perhaps you can try newly hatched fish or tad-

A bladderwort trap capturing a very young fish, whose yolk sac is not yet entirely absorbed

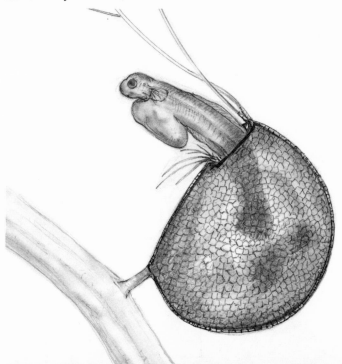

poles. You may be able to get infant guppies from a friend who has an excess in his tropical fish tank. Put a dozen baby guppies into your bladderwort aquarium and see if they are still alive next day.

You may be able to observe the actual trapping of a fish by a bladderwort trap. If you do, be sure to make accurate notes. Not many people have seen the actual capture, although many have seen the traps with fish caught in them.

If bladderworts can catch fish, are they a menace to fish hatcheries? Simms, the original observer, reported in 1884 that he had put about 150 newly hatched fish into a glass vessel containing bladderworts. Two days later only two or three of the tiny fish were still swimming about. Numbers of others were seen to be held fast in the traps by the head, by the tail, or by both head and tail.

Obviously the bladderwort plant can be quite destructive to young fish in confined quarters. Where fish and plants are crowded together in an aquarium, contact with the bladders takes place quite often. A baby fish need only touch the trigger hairs with a flick of its tail or a bump of its nose and it is sucked into the trap and gripped tight. If the fish is too small and weak to break away, it is bound to die.

Still, nobody can say whether this would happen in nature. With lots of room to swim around, the infant fish would seem to be reasonably safe. Occasionally one might get caught, but captures in a

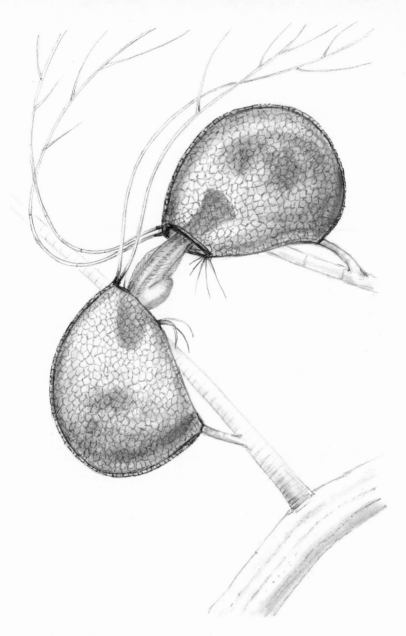

Occasionally one young fish is caught by two traps at the same time.

pond or lake must be less frequent than in a crowded aquarium.

Since bladderworts are such efficient trappers, it has been suggested that they could be used for mosquito control. The suggestion is based on the fact that mosquitos lay their eggs in water. The eggs hatch into larvae called wrigglers because they swim about with a peculiar wriggling motion. Wrigglers are frequently caught and destroyed in bladderwort traps.

This idea has already been tested. One experimenter put some bladderwort into a horse trough. Usually the water in such a trough is an excellent breeding place for mosquitos. But with bladderwort in the trough, every mosquito larva was destroyed. Next he put rafts of mosquito eggs into an aquarium containing bladderwort. He says that within two or three days after the eggs hatched, all the larvae were caught in the traps. No adult mosquitos ever came out of that aquarium.

The experimenter concluded that using bladderwort is a natural, practical method for mosquito control. He pointed out that chemical insect killers may destroy mosquito larvae, but they also kill practically all the life in the pond, including grown fish. However, badderworts placed in the water might destroy mostly mosquito larvae.

The logic sounds good, but the idea needs experiment—perhaps yours. Once again, will it work in the wide-open spaces of nature as well as it does in a confined aquarium or a barrel? Will it work in a pond or lake?

11
The Fish That Goes Fishing

We all know people that love to go fishing. Sometimes we call them anglers. They use various baits and lures to attract the fish. There is nothing unusual about a man who traps fish. But did you know that there are fish that go fishing? These anglerfish have their own built-in lures. Any fish that follows the lure of the anglerfish ends up in a trap from which there is no return.

Anglerfish are distributed all over the world. Let us describe one kind that is also called "the fishing frog." This is a rather large fish that may reach a length of six feet. But when you look at it, you may almost think you see only a head and tail, with no body in between. You get this impression because the fish has a huge head that is very wide, and flattened like the head of a toad. Its outstanding feature is an enormous, gaping mouth filled with rows of sharply pointed teeth. The mouth seems to take up the whole head. It looks even bigger because it is surrounded by a fringed border that looks like frilly lace.

This is one of the deep-sea anglerfish, Borophryne apogon. *There is a surprising variety in their strange "fishing lures."*

The fringe is continued back along the edges of the body. This gives the impression that the mouth, too, extends all the way back toward the tail. We can hardly blame people for saying that the anglerfish is "nothing but head and tail." However, you can rest assured that there is a body in between. In fact the stomach is so large that it can comfortably contain a young shark.

The eyes of this fish sit on top of the broad head, looking upward. Between the eyes is a filament that can be folded back or made to stand erect. This filament is really a part of the dorsal, or upper, fin. But in the anglerfish it has been modified into a "fishing rod." The top of the filament carries a small scrap of skin that glitters as it is moved through the water. Some anglerfish have two or three such filaments with glittering tips instead of just one.

The glittering tips are the lures that draw the victims to the trap—a very well disguised trap. The fish lies partly buried in the muddy sand at the bottom. Its color blends with the sand. The disguise is helped

DR. WILLIAM M. STEPHENS

Head-on view of the batfish, which inhabits tropical waters. The depression between its eyes contains a wormlike lure that it can bring out and dangle in front of its head.

by the fringed border that ornaments the mouth and sides; it softens the outline of the fish so that it merges into the background. For fishes passing overhead the trap is practically invisible.

Meanwhile the anglerfish is staring upward with its big eyes. As soon as it spots some passing fish, it raises the filaments and jerks them back and forth. This catches the attention of the prey. The curious fish are attracted by the glittering objects dancing about in the water. Maybe it is something good to eat? They come over to investigate. When the prey is close to the lure, the anglerfish suddenly heaves its immense head upward. The gaping mouth opens wide and the visiting fish is gulped in. Once inside the mouth there is no escape. The swordlike teeth point backward. There is only one direction for the victim to go— toward the stomach.

Anglerfish stay close to home most of the time. But for mating they swim long distances to their spawning grounds, which are underwater valleys as deep as five or six thousand feet. Here each female produces millions of eggs embedded in a jelly-like substance. The eggs float about in sheets that may be 20 to 30 feet long.

There are many other fish that use lures that entice victims to a trap. Perhaps the most interesting are the ones that live in the deepest parts of the ocean, where sunlight never penetrates. Many of these deep-sea fish carry their own special light-producing organs. In some cases these private lighting systems are apparently used to brighten the darkness where the fish swim, or to identify friends and foes. But in some of the deep-sea fish the light organs fool other fish, and lead them toward a deadly trap.

For example, the black sea devil is only an inch or two in length, but it is a competent angler. The first ray, or spine, of its dorsal fin carries a little lantern. It is pushed forward and shines brightly in the darkness. Many small creatures of the depths are attracted to this light, only to become victims of the traplike mouth that opens to swallow them.

A longlure frogfish, one of the many that can project a frilly filament from the front of its head as a "bait" for other fish. The fishing lure is one of the most interesting kinds of adaptation to be found in the seas.

Or consider the shining-tooth anglerfish. This one is completely invisible in the darkness except for its illuminated face that seems to grin. It is almost like the face of the Cheshire Cat of *Alice in Wonderland*. Perhaps you remember the story. The cat could fade out, leaving its grinning face hanging in midair. In the case of this anglerfish the face seems to be suspended in midwater. The only things visible are a pair of shining eyes, a dangling lantern, and a curving row of shining lights. The row of lights is really a mouthful of teeth. But how can a curious fish know this until it is too late?

Then there is the great gulper eel. This is a large fish, up to six feet long. It lures fish to its trap with a flaming red light organ near the tip of its tail. And there is the viper fish whose mouth contains several hundred light organs. These irresistible beacons draw many a shrimp or small fish right into the mouth.

12
The Death Pit

"Walk into my pitcher," whispers Nepenthes enticingly to the ant. "Follow the trail that I have spread for you. Who knows what wonders you will find at the end of it?"

This is of course a silent sort of whisper, since Nepenthes is a plant. But it can give off a perfume that can strongly attract an ant. Soon the insect is crawling along a trail of sweet nectar on one of its leaves.

It does not know that the fluid is really the bait for a trap, a death-pit from which there is no return. The ant follows the trail until it reaches the rim of a deep cup hanging at the end of the leaf. Here the sweet fragrance is stronger than ever. The trail goes over the top and starts down inside the cup.

The ant hesitates a moment. It puts forth a tentative leg but draws it back again. Still, the attraction is strong. The ant ventures a few steps along the trail. It can go downward without trouble. But if it turns around to climb back up, the path is barred by a forest of stiff hairs. These are like sharp spears pointing downward. And this is the only way the ant can go.

So it continues farther down the trail, lapping up the nectar as it goes. Now its footing becomes less secure. The inside walls of the cup are slick with wax. Suddeny there is no footing at all. The usually sure-footed insect begins to slip on the glassy surface. The hooks on its strong legs cannot grip these waxy walls. It tumbles downward to the bottom of the well and drops into a pool of clear fluid. This is the sweet wonder at the end of the trail. It is a narcotic that soon drugs the ant and quiets its struggles. And it is from this narcotic that the plant takes its name.

It is said that Egyptian doctors of long ago had a drug called nepenthe. A drink containing this drug quickly made a person forget all his troubles. According to the legend, it was nepenthe that helped Helen of Troy drown her sorrows when she fled to Egypt after the fall of Troy.

The fluid in the cup does more than put the ant to rest, however. It is also a mixture of enzymes that digest the tissues of the ant. Soon the tissues are converted into products that the plant can use for its own functions.

Actually, Nepenthes is the name applied to a whole group of pitcher plants, not just to a single variety. They are known as pitcher plants because the end of each leaf carries a tempting container half full of liquid. The plants are native to the islands scattered over the Indian Ocean and the western Pacific. They thrive there in the tropical jungles and marshes. Sometimes they climb to the tops of tall trees. Some of the larger varieties have pitchers measuring 15-20 inches deep from rim to bottom. These may even capture small tree toads or chameleons in addition to insects.

Pitcher plants of this type also grow wild in places like Malaysia and Borneo. You can often see them displaying their brilliant red and green pitchers in hothouses or botanic gardens in the United States. However, here in North America we have our own native types of pitcher plants. They may not be as large and showy as their tropical relatives, but they are just as efficient at trapping insects.

The North American plants have a long history. Fossil traces of these plants have been found in the rocks of the Cretaceous Period, when dinosaurs roamed the earth. Man did not yet exist. But pitcher plants were, we assume, capturing insects in those dim, distant days just exactly as they do today.

About fifteen living varieties inhabit the bogs and wet pinelands of North America. Sometime during the 1600s, Dr. M. S. Sarrazin of Quebec became interested in pitcher plants. He thought they might have some value in medicine because the local Indians sometimes used them in their herb remedies. Dr. Sarrazin sent specimen plants to Europe so trained botanists could study them. They were quite new to the European naturalists. In honor of Dr. Sarrazin, they named the plant Sarracenia.

Sarracenia purpurea, *one of the pitcher plants, with its death-trap leaves*

This is the commonest type of pitcher plant growing in eastern North America. It produces red-purple flowers that nod about a foot above a rosette of curved evergreen leaves. Each leaf is about five inches long when mature, and bears a pitcher at the end. The lip of the pitcher is covered with nectar glands.

An American type of pitcher plant makes an unusual house plant. It is evergreen, so its leaves (and their pitchers) stay on all through the winter. You can buy such plants from the sources mentioned in the footnote of Chapter 5. They are easy to grow.

The one important thing to remember is that the roots must never be allowed to dry. These plants

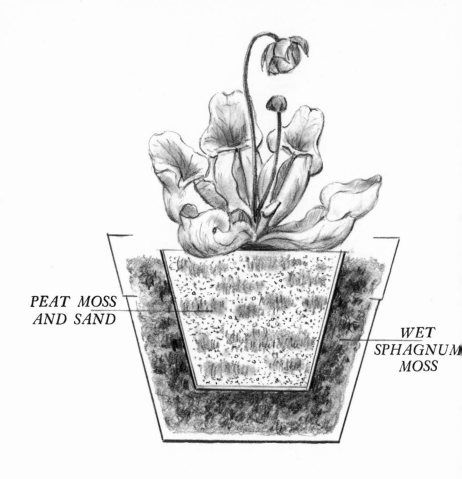

PEAT MOSS
AND SAND

WET
SPHAGNUM
MOSS

To grow a pitcher plant, put it in a clay pot filled with peat moss and sand. The outer pot, containing wet sphagnum moss, keeps the roots properly moist.

prosper in wet marshes and bogs. So root the pitcher plant in a clay flower pot containing a mixture of peat moss and sand. Put this pot into a larger pot, and stuff sphagnum moss in the space between the two pots. Keep the sphagnum moss wet at all times. The water will seep through the clay pot into the peat-sand mixture and keep the roots wet.

Pitcher plants make excellent subjects for observation and experiment. You can study them in the field if you are not afraid to get your feet wet. Or you can work with domesticated pitcher plants raised at home or in the school laboratory. In either case get yourself a notebook and write down everything you do, and everything you see. There are many interesting questions to explore.

For example, can an insect learn anything from its experiences in being lured into a pitcher plant? One biologist exposed a bluebottle fly to a Sarracenia. The fly was soon attracted by the nectar and climbed an erratic path to the rim, followed it, and fell into the pit. Now comes the most interesting part. The biologist cut a small window out of the wall of the pitcher. This allowed the fly to escape from the trap. You would think it had learned its lesson. But not so. It went right back to sipping nectar and fell in once more. This performance was repeated over and over again.

The fluid in the pitcher plant is an interesting subject for study. We know that it is death to insects, but it has been shown to be harmless to man. During an exploration trip in the tropics during the nineteenth century, Alfred Wallace drank some of it. His comment was: "We found it very palatable, though rather warm, and we all quenched our thirst from these natural jugs." More recently, in 1964, another explorer returning from Malaysia, the land of giant pitcher plants, said, "I found that immature pitchers still sealed by their caps contained the best-tasting water. It resembled in taste the water from the giant bamboos. The gluey fluid near the bottom of the cup was less appetizing. Drinkable in an emergency, I should say, but hardly recommended for routine use."

And here is a very interesting speculation for history buffs. In 1513 Ponce de Leon landed near where St. Augustine, Florida, stands today. This is pitcher plant territory. While searching for the elusive Fountain of Youth, surely he tried every fluid that came his way. What powers did Ponce de Leon and his crew find in the liquid of these flowering fly-catchers?

The fluid of the pitcher plant is worthy of your attention. It is not suggested that you taste it. But there are many questions to answer. For example: Does a young pitcher contain fluid? Where does the fluid come from? Is it rainwater that has accumulated? Is it fluid that is secreted by the cells of the plant? How would you find the answers to these questions?

Here are others: Can the pitcher plant fluid really digest something? Suppose you take some of the fluid out of the pitcher; will it still work in a test tube or a glass jar? Will it digest a speck of meat or hard-boiled egg white? Will it change starch into glucose (sugar)?

And still another: What kinds of animals make their homes in the pitcher plant fluid? The fluid may contain protozoa, worms, crustaceans, mosquito larvae, spiders, and even tadpoles—alive. These animals are most unusual, for they seem to be immune to the juices in which they swim. Nobody knows why they should be immune, while other very similar animals are soon killed and digested. They must have some hereditary protection that enables them to live, feed, and grow in the deadly fluid. Some of these animals feed on the tissues of the plant. Others feed on the insects that fall in.

One small red spider is known to spin a web just above the waterline in the pitcher. The spider then sits back and waits for insects to drop into the web. However, if it is disturbed or threatened, it dives into the fluid and hides there until the danger is past. This particular spider is not harmed by its dip in the poisonous pool, but other kinds of spiders are not immune.

Some of the animals that live in the pitcher plant fluid are found nowhere else in the world. You can see some of them for yourself, if you have a microscope and a lot of patience. Examine a few drops of pitcher plant fluid under the microscope. Do you find any living organisms? How many kinds? Are any of them visible to the naked eye? Are they present in young pitchers, or only in mature pitchers? How do you think they get there? Does the population change from time to time as the pitcher grows older?

13
A Lasso for an Eelworm

The next time you stroll in the country, give a little thought to the mysterious world beneath your feet. You are stepping on soil that makes up the topmost layer of our earth. It is really just a thin skin covering what lies below. But that skin holds many strange mysteries worthy of exploration.

It is just dirt, but what is dirt to you is home and life to millions of small living things. Some of them are plants; others are animals. They all live down there in that dirt. As you walk along you are actually stepping on the roof of their home.

Theirs is a world of total darkness. It is a world of sand and stone and gravel. It is a world shot through with air spaces and dark tunnels that twist and turn in every direction. When it rains, these channels conduct the water down to the lower depths. Here and there the growing root of a plant pokes its way through the darkness.

Many members of the hidden population never see the light of day. Still, they feed, they grow, they reproduce—for generation after generation. Somehow they have become adjusted to life in the soil.

These organisms have developed many strange adaptations that help them live successfully. There is even a group of trappers among them. They are microscopic plants that produce a marvelous variety of snares. Any small worm that comes in contact with one of these traps becomes food for the silent trapper. Usually these are microscopic roundworms. They belong to an animal group called the nematodes. These little animals are found almost everywhere—in the soil, in fresh water, in salt water, inside the bodies of plants and animals.

If all the matter of our earth were swept away except the nematodes, our world would still be faintly recognizable. We could still make out the outlines of mountains, hills, valleys, rivers, lakes, oceans, and even forests. A thin, ghostly film of nematodes would remain to show us where all these places used to be. This idea is not new. It was suggested many years ago by a world-famous expert on nematodes.

For the moment we will concentrate on those that live in the soil. Here we find them by the millions. Some are free-living roundworms that move among the soil particles. Others are parasitic roundworms that live on the roots of plants, or in the very plant tissues. It is estimated that a cubic yard of soil may contain as many as twenty million living nematodes.

The soil nematodes swim in the delicate film of water that surrounds every soil particle. They whip about with a peculiar motion that makes them easy to recognize. In a way it resembles the twisting and turning of an eel. For this reason they are often referred to as eelworms.

The trapper that snares these worms is a microscopic member of a large group of plants known as the fungi. They are nongreen plants, so they cannot manufacture their own food; they must draw nourishment from outside sources.

Some of them are parasites—they get their food by invading the bodies of living animals or plants. Among them are disease bacteria, the fungus of athlete's foot, the fungus that causes wheat rust, and so on. The others get their food by breaking down organic substances. They feed on the dead bodies of animals or plants, decaying leaves, bread, cheese, and other comparable materials. They include such forms as decay bacteria, bread mold, penicillium mold, and yeasts.

Our trappers are fungi that have found a special way to supplement their diet: they set traps to capture living eelworms. They can live perfectly well without doing this, but every extra bit of food helps. One can't really call them parasites, because they get their own food. Biologists refer to them as predaceous fungi, which simply means that they are fungi that capture prey.

The body of such a fungus is similar to those of other molds. It consists of a network of branching filaments, filled with living matter. New threads can grow out at any point on the network. As the tip of a new thread grows forward, the living matter streams into it. By producing new threads, the mold spreads and invades new territories.

Different kinds of eelworm-trappers produce different kinds of traps. In its simplest form, the trap is only a secretion of some kind of mucilage. Imagine an eelworm wriggling about violently, as eelworms do. By accident it bumps into the mold filament. Suddenly it finds itself stuck fast to the glue.

Other trappers have snares that are a little more complicated, and therefore a little more efficient. They may produce special groups of sticky knobs someone has called "lethal lollipops." Or they may have clusters of rings and loops that are coated with mucilage. If an

The fungus Arthrobotrys conoides *forms clusters of sticky loops.*

DR. DAVID PRAMER

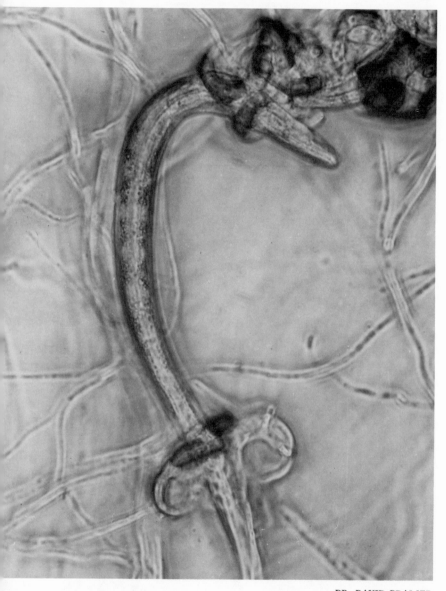

A nematode trapped by the gluey network of the fungus.

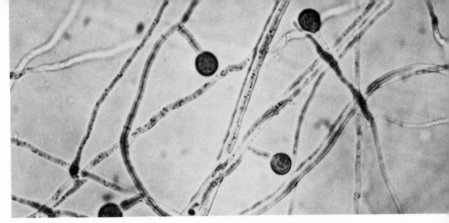

The fungus Dactylella drechsleri *produces "lollipops," or adhesive knobs.*

eelworm touches the knobs or wanders into the loops, he has no hope for escape. He is trapped as surely as the fly that is dancing on flypaper.

The most highly developed traps resemble tiny lassos. Each one is made of three cells, arranged in a circle. The center is open. The ring sits up on a little stalk, at right angles to the rest of the filament. If a wandering nematode sticks its head into one of these rings, the three cells expand instantly. The open space in the middle of the ring becomes smaller, and in less than a tenth of a second the eelworm has a collar tightened about it. It is as though it had put its head into a lasso and somebody pulled it tight.

This special lasso is just the right size. Nobody understands exactly how it works, but it is a hundred per cent effective. No eelworm ever escapes. Even if it succeeds in breaking away, it swims off with a collar of fungus around it. The result is still the same.

The worm struggles for a while but soon becomes quiet. Does the fungus produce a chemical that

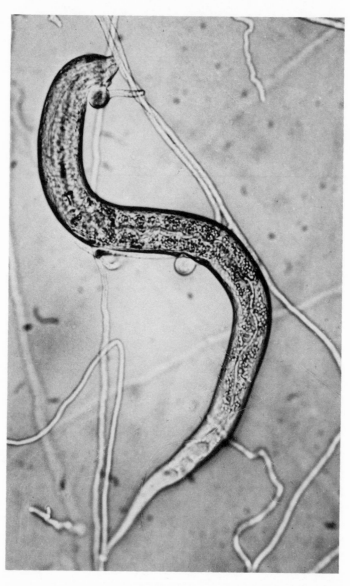

A nematode has brushed against two of the knobs and become stuck.

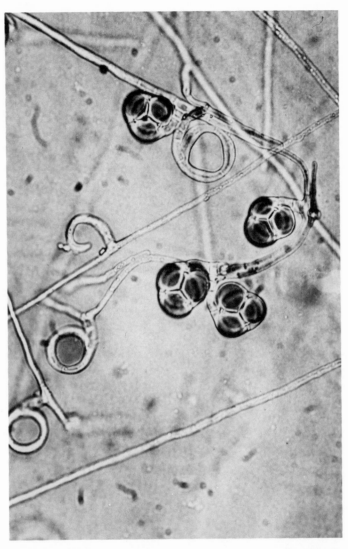

Another type of fungus, Arthrobotrys dactyloides, *produces* "lassos." *When these are touched, the cells of which they are made swell instantly, as can be seen in the case of the four darkish lassos, which are now closed.*

kills? Nobody really knows. However, as soon as the worm is quiet, the fungus begins to work. A fine filament of the plant penetrates the worm at the point where it is held. Once inside, it swells up into a bulb. New branches grow out of the bulb and spread to every part of the worm's body.

Now enzymes are produced that digest the tissues of the worm. The useful products are absorbed by the threads of the fungus. In about 24 hours the job of digestion and absorption is completed. Soon the living material of the fungus begins to pull back. It streams out of the worm back to the main body of the plant, carrying along all the useful nutrients that it absorbed. Only the dead walls of the empty fungus threads are left behind inside the empty skin of the worm.

A nematode has put its head in one of the lassos and been trapped.

DR. DAVID PRAMER

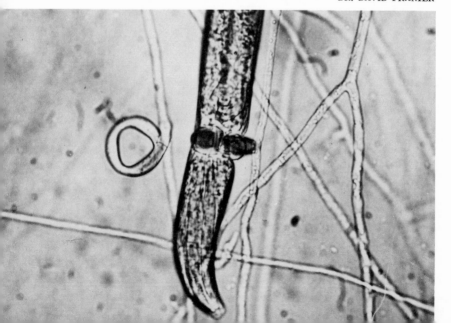

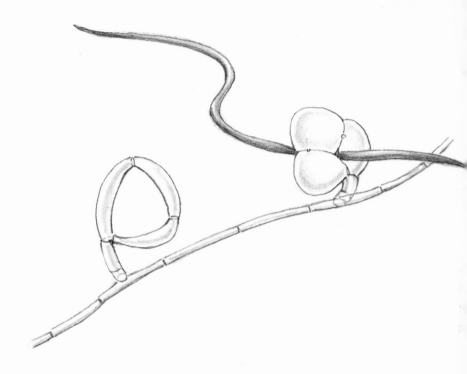

A view of the lasso showing the three long cells clearly when in the open state, and how they round out into three "pillows" as they expand into a killing collar.

Would you agree that these traps are a marvelous adaptation? But wait. There is still a mystery for you to solve, if you can. It has been shown that lasso traps are never produced unless eelworms are nearby. How does the fungus "know" when prey is available and when it is not? Some biologists think that the eelworms themselves give the signal, that they give off some special chemical that sets off the fungus. That is their theory. What's yours?

Suggested Reading

Here is a selected list of readings for those who want additional information about the trappers described in this book. Some of these references were written for older people, but you can find a great deal of interest if you read them.

ADAPTATION

Burnett, Allison L., and Thomas Eisner, *Animal Adaptation* (Holt, N.Y., 1964; in Modern Biology Series)

Wallace, Bruce, and Adrian M. Srb, *Adaptation* (Prentice-Hall, Englewood Cliffs, N.J., 1964; in Foundations of Modern Biology Series)

Zuidema, L. W., "The Changeable Snowshoe Hare," *The Conservationist* (N. Y. S. Conservation Department, Albany, N.Y.), Feb./Mar. 1970

PLANTS THAT TRAP ANIMALS (IN GENERAL)

Argo, V. N., "Insect-Trapping Plants," *Natural History*, March 1964

Lloyd, F. E., *The Carnivorous Plants* (Ronald Press, N.Y., 1942)

Poole, Lynn, and Gray Poole, *Insect-Eating Plants* (T. Y. Crowell, N.Y., 1963)

Zahl, P. A., "Plants That Eat Insects," *National Geographic*, May 1961

ANT LIONS

Herbert, Hiram J., "Insect of Prey—The Story of the Wily Ant Lion, Master Strategist," *Nature Magazine*, Feb. 1936

Krutch, J. W., "Unnatural History of the Ant Lion," *Natural History*, March 1968

Rozen, J. G., and B. L. Rozen, "Pit-Digging Predator," *Natural History*, Mar. 1962 (Excellent photos of the ant lion are included.)

VENUS'S-FLYTRAP

Anon., "Venus's Fly Trap in Action," *Nature Magazine*, March 1937

Deans, E. V., "Venus's Fly Trap," *Nature Magazine*, July 1936

CADDIS WORMS

Hutchins, Ross E., *Caddis Insects: Nature's Carpenters and Stonemasons* (Dodd, Mead, N.Y., 1966)

SPIDERS

Dugdale, B. E., "Weaving of an Engineering Masterpiece," *Natural History*, March 1969 (Weaving an orb web)

Jenks, George E., "The Birth of a Baby Black Widow," *Natural History*, June 1938

Lougee, L. B., "How to Collect and Preserve Webs of Spiders," *Scientific American*, Feb. 1963 (In the Amateur Scientist section conducted by C. L. Stong.)

Kaston, B. J., and E. Kaston, *How to Know the Spiders* (Wm. C. Brown Co., Dubuque, Iowa, 1953; available in paperback).

Palmer, E. L., "Spiders and Webs," *Natural History*, Oct. 1961

Romane, M., "Joys of Culturing Spiders and Investigating Their Webs," *Scientific American*, Dec. 1972 (In the Amateur Scientist section conducted by C. L. Stong.)

Zahl, P. A., "What's So Special about Spiders?" *National Geographic*, Aug. 1971 (Includes beautiful color photographs.)

SUNDEWS

Ashley, T., and J. F. Gennaro, "Fly in the Sundew," *Natural History*, Dec. 1971 (Describes use of radioactive substances to follow the digestive process of the sundew. Good photos.)

Eisner, T., "Life on the Sticky Sundew," *Natural History*, June 1967 (Describes a caterpillar that makes its home on the sundew.)

HYDRAS

Berrill, N. J., "The Indestructible Hydra," *Scientific American*, Dec. 1957 (Describes ability of the hydra to grow back missing parts.)

Burnett, A. L., "Hydra: An Immortal's Nature," *Natural History*, Nov. 1959

Goldstein, Philip, "The Indestructible Hydra," Section I of the book *Triumphs of Biology* (Doubleday, Garden City, N.Y., 1965. Historical background on hydra)

———, "Things to Do With Hydra," Section 4 of the book *Experiments with Microscopic Animals*, with Jerome Metzner (Doubleday, Garden City, N.Y., 1971. Activities with hydra that a student can carry on at home or in the school laboratory.)

BLADDERWORTS

Gudger, E. W., "The Only Known Fish-Catching Plant," *Scientific Monthly*, May 1947

ANGLERFISH

Heinold, George, "The Fisherman with a Built-in Lure," *Science Digest*, Jan. 1970.

Idyll, C. P., *Abyss: The Deep Sea and the Creatures That Live in It* (T. Y. Crowell, N.Y., 1964)

Severin, Kurt, "Just to Change the Subject," *Outdoor Life*, Oct. 1966 (Has underwater shots showing anglerfish using its lure.)

PITCHER PLANTS

Zahl, P. A., "Malaysia's Giant Flowers and Insect-Trapping Plants," *National Geographic*, May 1964 (Beautiful color photos.)

Duddington, C. L., *The Friendly Fungi* (Faber & Faber, London, 1957)

Pramer, David, and N. Dondero, "Microscopic Traps," *Natural History*, Dec. 1957 (Includes excellent photos and drawings of the traps in action.)

Maio, Joseph J., "Predatory Fungi," *Scientific American*, July 1958 (Offprint #1094)

Index